# What people are saying about Journaling Power

"*Journaling Power* is a candid, beautifully-written self-help book, filled with warmth, wit and wisdom."

~ Dennis Palumbo, psychotherapist and author,
*Writing From The Inside Out*

"Remarkable, riveting and transformative. These are the three words that I believe best describe Mari's exceptional book. Whether you journal or not, whether you have even thought about journaling or not, you will definitely want to dive in to discover how this one simple process can radically and positively impact your life in many ways. Highly recommended."

~ Peggy McColl, New York Times best-selling author

"Mari shows amazing courage and resourcefulness in tackling her illness head-on and using all her inner resources to unwind its psychological underpinnings. She writes with full personal transparency, and using herself as the vehicle, she clearly and powerfully instructs and inspires the reader in the art of journaling. Of course you don't have to have a life-threatening illness like MS to reap the benefits of this beautifully-written and most inspiring book. All that being said, as a functional medicine physician, I cheered when she all-too-briefly mentioned going gluten and dairy free, since we look for underlying causes and in such autoimmune illnesses as MS, focus on gut health, gluten and other sensitivities, and lack of such nutrients as vitamin D."

~ Hyla Cass, M.D., nationally acclaimed expert in integrative medicine, psychiatry, and addiction recovery, associate editor of *Total Health Magazine*, and best-selling Author of *8 Weeks to Vibrant Health*

D1502652

"Mari's approach to journaling brings to mind the Taoist idea of Radiant Health – which is possible only when we cultivate wellbeing of the mind and body and an adaptability to the stresses of the world around us. After reading this book, I plan to add journaling to my doctor's bag right alongside Jing herbs for their power to heal the body, mind and spirit.

~ George Lamoureux, DAOM, LAc – Qi Gong Master, Founder and CEO of Jing Herbs, and best-selling author of *High Performance Entrepreneurs Handbook: 5 Easy Recipes for Maintaining Energy, Productivity, Immunity and Well-Being*

"Journaling Power is a wonderful book that helps us connect with our abilities to heal the mind, body and spirit."

~ Sally Schutz, M.D., Lyme Disease Expert and best-selling Author of *The Anti-Aging Miracles of Hemp Derived CBD Oil*

"If you've ever doubted the therapeutic and transformative benefits of journaling, you need to read Mari L. McCarthy's *Journaling Power*. Mari shares her intense physical struggle with MS; the emotional decision to close her consulting business, which was her identity at the time; and goes to battle with her Inner Critic in a remarkable healing journey that transforms her life physically, psychologically, and spiritually. She not only shares her personal story and stories from the CreateWriteNow community but also the medical evidence and science behind the benefits of journaling. Journaling is the wonder drug that Big Pharma doesn't want you to know about! A powerful tool for positive change, this book also contains the inspirational journaling exercises and encouragement that Mari is famous for, so you can embark on your own journey of transformation."

~ Angela Mackintosh, *WOW! Women On Writing*

"Mari delivers all that she promises and more in *Journaling Power: How to Create the Healthy, Happy Life You Want to Live.* Through accessible language and well-illustrated practices, she shares physical and emotional challenges she successfully managed along her journey to become the woman she aspires to be. You will find dozens of writing suggestions and a straightforward guideline for establishing your own writing practice. As a reader interested in evidenced-based expressive writing practices, I am delighted she supports her claims for *Journaling Power* with a good number of highly regarded studies and will suggest this book to my clients who wish to begin writing to make life course corrections."

~ John Evans, executive director, Wellness & Writing Connections

"I've interviewed hundreds of people offering their stories about the benefits of keeping a journal. But the most profound story of them all, illustrating the healing power of writing (on the physical as well as emotional, professional, and intellectual levels), is that of Mari L. McCarthy. Her journey is inspiring, and demonstrates how to love one's body in the pursuit of self-understanding. Her no-nonsense advice for starting a journaling routine is transformative."

~ Nathan Ohren, best-selling author,
and host of the *JournalTalk* podcast.

"With a raw honesty, Mari conveys the physical and emotional challenges that compelled her to courageously explore new ways to heal and transform herself. Reading her book is like observing the evolution of a passionate relationship – with journaling! You'll want to use that famous line from *When Harry Met Sally* – "I'll have what she's having." We meet Inner Critic and Inner Coach, and are given a sprinkling of thought-provoking quotes and enriching journaling exercises. You'll feel inspired by a woman whose courage and passion not only enabled her to heal and transform herself in body, mind, and spirit, but go on to make her life work helping others do the same."

~ Joan Leof, author and memoirist

# JOURNALING POWER

## HOW TO CREATE THE HAPPY, HEALTHY LIFE **YOU** WANT TO LIVE

Mari L. McCarthy

*The only disability in life is a bad attitude.*

– Scott Hamilton

*Challenges are opportunities requesting action.*

– Mari L. McCarthy

To my main music men, Perry Rossi, Justin Stoney, David Stephenson, and Dominic Devitt, who taught me to think with my heart and sing from my soul.

To Lyn Alderson, my soul sister, for her love, inspiration, and adult supervision.

# Table of Contents

# Introduction

*I hear and I forget, I see and I remember,*
*I write and I understand.*

– Chinese Proverb

B ack in 1998 I did not have the strength to cook a meal without dropping my saucepans (and sometimes my dinner) on the kitchen floor, and I had very little function in the right side of my body. I had been floored, quite literally, by an ongoing health crisis.

As a successful consultant advising Fortune 1000 companies, I had previously owned my own business, but I'd been forced to sell it due to my disability. I wasn't even able to write my name properly, as I'd lost the use of my right hand. A few years earlier, I'd regularly walked for miles just for fun and fitness; I'd been quite athletic as a young person, a good sprinter and basketball player. Now I could no longer walk down the street in a straight line; in the eyes of people who didn't know me, I looked exactly like the town drunk. Things couldn't get much worse for the girl who had once solved everyone else's problems.

In a desperate bid to recover my health I was following conventional medical advice, and taking a cocktail of prescription drugs every day as I dutifully went from one specialist to another. But my condition was getting worse instead of better. It took a mammoth effort every day to coordinate my legs and walk from the bedroom to the bathroom. I felt diminished by my chronic illness.

I needed a radical transformation, and it came when a friend introduced me to writing therapy (also known as therapeutic journaling or expressive writing). At first I viewed journaling as a means to an end (I wanted to learn to write with my left hand) but I soon noticed how it eased my bodily symptoms, especially when I wrote about them in depth. Before I started journaling about the lack of function in my right side, for example, I'd been suffering a lot with numbness and tingling in the affected areas. My right arm was colder and redder in appearance than my left arm, but over a period of time the blood flow improved and my affected arm began to look normal. Gradually the generalized numbness and tingling I felt on my right side diminished too. I also noticed improvements in my digestion after writing about my rushed approach to mealtimes and implementing some changes in my eating habits.

As I continued to explore my physical and emotional distress through journaling, I realized I'd been abusing my body for years and ignoring its cries for help. I'd driven it recklessly like an automobile, yet it was actually a living organism in need of care and attention. I started to take a holistic approach to my health and introduced some lifestyle changes.

Right from day one, journaling revealed my issues and helped me find solutions. I was forced to recognize my negative self-image and to discover that I hadn't dealt with the pain of my childhood. With my journal as a catalyst, I began a metamorphosis, a dynamic process of physical, emotional, and spiritual change. After a year or two of regular writing therapy I found I didn't need the masses of prescription drugs I'd been taking, so I stopped buying insurance and saved myself thousands of dollars a year. (I'm not saying everyone should do this, but it worked for me.)

However, the biggest surprise of all was this: through journaling I had found a door into my soul.

I began to discover who the real Mari L. McCarthy was: an individual with unfulfilled dreams that had somehow been forgotten and buried; a person with innate talents that had not been recognized or developed. My journal entries revealed what mattered to the real me, and the path I needed to take. As I got in touch with my deepest thoughts, feelings, and desires, I began to change my whole way of life. I learned to think with my heart and not just my head.

Before I started journaling, I was dominated by my left brain. I was always practical, logical, and rational, and I thought that showing emotion was a sign of weakness. This had a lot to do with how I'd been raised. I'd been taught to keep a stiff upper lip and did so 24/7 (I never even cried over the death of my mother, whom I loved dearly). But through reflective writing I began to understand that my feelings were important and must be heard. I realized I could engage with the business world and yet be creative in my approach, maintaining a healthy, balanced lifestyle that allowed me to be myself.

This transformation in attitude and behavior was not an overnight miracle; it involved hard work and soul-searching on my part, but it brought measurable results and success in the external world. Soon, I had a future that excited me: I seized my life back, regained significant function in the right side of my body, started an online journaling community, and then I really surprised myself – I learned to sing and became a recording artist! These were major achievements that combined to give me the life I longed for; journaling was a very specific and effective toolkit to facilitate them.

Today I am happy and fulfilled. I feel healthy and sleep soundly. I work from my beachfront home near Boston, running my second successful business, enjoying a quality of life I once thought impossible. It has been such an amazing journey that I feel compelled to share it with you. This is a book that HAD to be written. It would have been wrong to keep my story all to myself.

So in these pages I want to share my experience of writing therapy (or Journaling Power as I like to call it), the self-help therapy that changed my life. I will give you all of the knowledge and tools you need to start a journal-writing practice of your own. If you use them daily, you can expect to see big changes in your life.

The benefits of journaling are multi-faceted, and vary between individuals. If you have a chronic illness, you may find that the symptoms become less troublesome. Expressive writing has helped people suffering with asthma, rheumatoid arthritis, IBS, and lupus – even cancer and AIDS. It helps many people with different long-term illnesses, because it boosts the immune system. This book evaluates and presents the medical evidence for journaling, which has been steadily growing over the past thirty years.

If your life is highly pressured, journaling is an excellent stress-management tool. Stress is a huge factor in many physical and mental health problems and compromises the immune system. Therapeutic writing appears to have a protective effect against stress and possibly acts as a release valve.

One of the pioneers of writing therapy, research psychologist Dr. James Pennebaker from the University of Texas, has carried out numerous scientific studies. He found that a few sessions of expressive writing can have a beneficial effect for months, resulting in fewer visits to the doctor. Many other academics have developed and expanded his work with positive outcomes.

A review published in the *British Journal of General Practice* in 2012 concluded writing therapy can potentially help thirty percent of patients who visit the doctor in primary care settings and could be used potentially "very widely indeed." In a separate review in the Royal College of Psychiatrists' journal *Advances in Psychiatric Treatment*, UK clinical psychiatrist Kay Wilhelm concludes that for some people expressive writing is "extremely helpful and has quickly resolved issues that have been mulled over – sometimes for years – with no resolution" (Baikie & Wilhelm, 2005). Many other U.S. studies support these conclusions, which you can read about in Chapter 7 of this book.

Journaling helps you manage your life and avoid burnout. If you have many responsibilities at work and at home, and have to juggle the needs of children or elderly parents with a demanding career, you can easily become weary. Paradoxically, therapeutic writing will help you avoid exhaustion by learning to prioritize tasks and care for your own needs holistically. You will learn to live life proactively and mindfully so that you are not just responding to each and every crisis with a knee-jerk reaction.

If you've recently experienced a specific trauma, such as a bereavement, divorce, or loss of your job, there is solid scientific evidence that expressive writing helps in recovery. In one social psychology experiment, researchers studied a group of middle-aged men who were angry about losing their jobs. They found that the men who were selected to take part in writing exercises to express their emotions were much more likely to find a new job than those who had not taken part in the writing tasks (Spera, Buhrfeind, & Pennebaker 1994).

Journaling increases our working-memory capacity (that's the short-term memory we use for problem solving and carrying out complex tasks). It can therefore make us more productive in our jobs as well as boost academic performance, as measured by exam grades. Expressive writing has been shown to lift moods and reduce depression, improve social relationships, and even enhance performance on the sports field!

The benefits of expressive writing are now well established in the scientific community. Dr. Pennebaker has commented, "As the number of studies increased, it became clear that writing was far more powerful than anyone ever dreamed."

So if journaling is a powerful therapy, why haven't we heard more about it? If it were a drug, it would have been marketed extensively by now and we would all know someone taking it. But the truth is, journaling is so simple and straightforward, it cannot be trademarked or patented. Large corporations can't find a way of making money out of it, so it's been largely ignored.

Writing by hand, with a pen and notebook, is also quite retro. Like meditation, it requires a reflective state of being, rather than doing. We have to step away from our highly stimulating modern environment with the distractions of social media, television, and mobile phones, back to something much more ancient and wise. Journaling is a form of in-depth narrative, and uses our capacity to tell stories. This storytelling is as old as the human race and runs counter to our sound-bite culture. So we have to make a special effort to engage in it initially.

After you've been doing it for a few weeks and reaping the benefits it will become a habit you won't want to break. And you'll learn to live differently, taking note of the still, small voice within that knows what you really want and need. There is an inner wisdom that we all have access to and a strength we can draw upon if we give ourselves the time to find this sacred space. The further you go on the journaling journey, the greater the harmony you will experience. Things fall into place and you will discover synchronization in your inner and outer life.

It's easy to start journaling once you've made up your mind; you only need a pen and a notebook, the information in this book, and the determination to write a little every day. Your journal will teach you the rest once you get started. You'll discover that it's the best therapist you could ever hope for – and it doesn't charge you a cent.

But don't let the simplicity of Journaling Power fool you. This is a powerful therapy. So powerful that I believe it's only a matter of time before writing therapy is recognized as a holistic therapy in its own right. Some doctors and mental health professionals already use it with their patients, because it's cost-effective, convenient, and as powerful as many of the medications commonly used today.

Have I said enough to convince you? Are you ready to commit to a healing process that takes just a few minutes a day? You may not think of yourself as a naturally gifted writer, but good English, spelling, and neat handwriting are irrelevant to journal therapy. Your journal is not for public consumption. It's the process of writing things down that brings about healing.

Because you may be new to journaling, I'd like to share my experience and offer you some encouragement. I was the most unlikely journaler when I started out – highly driven, impatient, and an expert at ignoring my feelings. If you'd known me in those days, you would never have expected me to take the time to journal on a daily basis. But once I experienced the benefits, I never looked back.

For the past eight years I have been the Chief Inspiration Officer at CreateWriteNow, the online community I set up to support journalers everywhere. I have seen the community grow into thousands of followers, and we have learned from each other through sharing our "journaling journeys." I offer myself as your personal transformation guide as you work through this book. I hope you enjoy reading my story and the brief testimonies of others who have been journaling for years.

Though a few authors have written about the virtues of journaling, this book is unique because it offers an in-depth case study and "how to" advice in one volume. You can also read the stories of like-minded people who trusted themselves to the journaling process. This book is not a dry academic tome listing endless scientific studies; rather, it offers practical exercises to help you apply simple principles to your own life. It invites you to form a close relationship with your new, completely trustworthy best friend. You can learn to live from the inside out, not just reacting to your circumstances, but proactively creating a happier, healthier, and more productive life.

## What to Expect

Here's what you can hope to receive from a daily, pen-to-paper journaling practice, if you follow Journaling Power guidelines:

- reduced stress, strain, and suffering – and quite possibly lower healthcare expenses

- a deeper understanding of yourself and the life experiences that have shaped you

- a healthier, more compassionate relationship with yourself, and an appreciation of your unique qualities, skills, and talents

- the ability to enjoy the present moment without worrying about the future or grieving over past mistakes

- resolution of inner conflict and improved relationships

- greater freedom in the creative process and an unlocking of power, talents, and abilities that were previously blocked

- the ability to face your fears and move forward in life

- motivation to care for yourself first, resulting in more energy to care for others

- the ability to set realistic goals and targets and make them happen

So find yourself a notebook and pen, and a quiet, comfortable, private space where no one will disturb you. Journaling is so easy you can get started on your transformation right away.

My goal in this book is to give you the knowledge, inspiration, and tools you need to create a happy, healthy life! Most of the chapters start with narrative, as I share my own journaling experiences with you, followed by advice on how to begin and maintain your journaling practice. Each chapter finishes with exercises to help you set sail on a lifelong voyage of discovery.

It's as simple as that! Welcome to the exciting, adventurous, inspiring world of Journaling Power.

**#WriteON!**

# My Wake-Up Call

*Every human being is the author of his own health or disease.*

– Swami Sivananda

It was bad news, I thought as I focused my eyes on the doctor sitting opposite me. He was holding an image taken from an MRI scan and his expression was kind, compassionate, and deadly serious. He pulled his chair toward me a little, so that I could see the black-and-white film more easily, and announced:

"Mari, your problem is all in your head. And I don't mean it's psychosomatic, or that you're imagining things. The problem is here, in your brain."

He indicated the scan, which showed the various regions of my brain, and I noticed that there were white spots all over it. What on earth were they?

Fear gripped my heart as terrifying thoughts torpedoed through my mind:

*Oh no, my beloved brain is broken!*

*How could it let me down like this? What will I do?*

*How will I run my life? I depend on my brain to do everything.*

My heart was thumping hard against my chest and I'd almost stopped breathing. I was preparing myself for the diagnosis that was surely coming. It was bound to be a brain tumor, my worst nightmare come true. How could I survive as a top business consultant if I had to have brain surgery? Worse still, was it going to be terminal?

Inside my head I screamed at my body for letting me down, while outwardly I nodded dutifully at Dr. Mouchatti and swallowed hard, pushing my emotions down.

I could feel a wet patch appearing under my arms as I clenched my jaw and bit hard on my lip to stop myself from crying. I forced myself to take a deep, deep breath and remain calm as I asked, "Is it a brain tumor?"

I waited for what seemed like an age for my neurologist's reply:

"Don't panic – you don't have a brain tumor, Mari. You have an auto-immune disease. These white spots are classic signs of multiple sclerosis."

Relief flooded through my body and mind. I'd heard of multiple sclerosis, and I knew it was a serious and potentially disabling condition. But it was not as bad as the scenarios I'd been imagining for the past five months as I'd crashed into the walls of my house and banged into doorways without knowing why.

*Whew,* I sighed, feeling my body relax. *It's only MS.*

*It isn't an incurable cancer. It isn't a death sentence. There is room for hope.*

"What happens now?" I asked Dr. Mouchatti, who had placed the MRI scan back into a file.

"Multiple sclerosis is a degenerative disease that affects people in different ways," he explained. "It affects nerve cells in the brain and spinal cord. Its impact on the nervous system can be severe, but in between flare-ups of the disease, symptoms can disappear. Surgery is not an option and there is no magic pill that will solve all of your problems."

"Then what can I do?" I asked.

"There's no known cause or cure," he said. "The best I can give you is a prescription to settle your physical symptoms – and I would recommend that you reduce stress."

As I left the clinic that Friday afternoon in 1991, the business-woman inside me took the reins. I got into my car and began working out a plan to tackle my newly diagnosed disease. It shouldn't be impossible to deal with this hurdle, not with my impeccable track record of solving problems. This could go right to the top of my "to do" list!

To stay positive I reminded myself of all my achievements to date.

I'd left college with a degree in journalism and taken a job in business right after graduation. I'd joined a big management-consulting group where I was one of only three female consultants among six hundred men. But I'd proved my worth; I came up with the solutions that people were looking for and climbed the corporate ladder.

Now I owned my own successful business consulting firm and lived life in the fast lane. The ultimate goal-setter, I took pride in moving the business forward, striving to be the best that I could be. I had achieved a lot in a short time. I was Mari, the Go-To Girl – and I could find the answer to almost any problem.

Driving home, I vowed I would not be beaten by this challenge, which now had a name. I would not let the balance sheet of my business suffer. I would spend the weekend drawing up an action plan for myself, just as I did quite often for my clients.

I got to work immediately. As I didn't have a cross-country plane to catch until Sunday afternoon, I sat and read everything I could about MS. I also scheduled some time to make modifications to how I ran my business. My role was demanding and my poor health had been affecting my performance; this was something I would not tolerate!

It was my role to help Fortune 1000 companies develop and improve their bottom line and I had a flair for it, which meant I was always in demand. My business partner, Mike, my staff, and I were busy working on about six projects located in some of the most inaccessible industrial regions of the USA. These locations – Kingsport, Tennessee; Trona, California; and Big Spring, Texas, to name a few – were not exactly garden spots. My life involved long airplane flights, trips on puddle jumpers, and then rental car drives of an hour on average. To get to Trona we were forced to take a scary flight on a puddle jumper into the mountains! It was grueling to rush backward and forward week after week between far-flung locations, but I had always accepted my punishing schedule as an inescapable part of the job.

Most of my weeks were spent at least partially on the move. I would get home late every Friday and barely had time to open my mail and do my laundry, before it was time to head back to the airport on Sunday evening. I had been running on pure adrenaline for years.

This fast-paced life had always given me a buzz, but lately my body had been flagging. I needed to reverse this decline.

For the past year I'd been exhausted for long stretches of my days; I also felt "left of center." It was as if I had been attacked on the right side of my body. My coordination was completely off. I'd raise an arm, reach for something, and waver. The side of my face seemed strangely desensitized; my leg felt not quite painful, but not quite pain-free. My sense of balance had deteriorated too.

Walking down the street – barreling my way to a meeting, running in high heels to meet a new client, or even just making my way home – I had started to teeter. A few weeks earlier, without warning, I'd lost my balance and collapsed at home. When I tried to get up, my legs would not support me, so I'd been forced to call the emergency services. They'd had to break down the door to pick me up off the floor!

My symptoms had been getting worse day by day. At the start of my illness I was not particularly anxious; I saw my fatigue and declining mobility as little more than an inconvenience. I was puzzled and surveyed my body with a mixture of curiosity and anger, constantly wondering, *How could it let me down like that?*

I told myself there must be a straightforward solution to my problems if only I could find the right specialist. I had kept myself going with iron willpower until finally Mike had insisted I took time off to get my health issues sorted out.

Immediately before my diagnosis I'd developed a fear that I had a brain tumor, but I now knew this wasn't the case, and this gave me renewed hope of a medical solution to my problems. Reviewing my decline over the past few months, I realized I would have to make practical changes until my condition improved. But I was determined to manage my newly diagnosed disease. I was prepared to follow whatever regimen my doctor put me on. I would deal decisively with this hurdle and then dive back in to my busy life.

I had always treated my body like a machine that needed only minimal attention. I knew I was supposed to exercise regularly, eat the right foods, and drink plenty of water. And I'd done all of those things as much as I could without much thought. But now I would have to dig deeper to find the best treatment, a regime that would ease my debilitating symptoms.

Even if the symptoms got worse, I would deal with them, one by one. I would stay on top of things and I would not let my quality of life or happiness, my hopes or my dreams, run down the drain.

I had always been fiercely determined about issues I cared about – taking care of my siblings, for instance, or getting the grades or the profit margins I wanted – and this time the level of determination was just as strong. But now there was a big difference: my determination turned toward myself. To "succeed" in *this* challenge, I would have to stay attuned to my health. I was in a situation that demanded steely determination; I had no other choice. I knew that if I didn't take control, things would overwhelm me. And I decided right away that I would become my primary caregiver, and put myself first out of necessity.

## Dealing with Disease

After modifying my activities a little, I made appointments to see the best doctors. I went to see a number of specialists and obeyed all of their instructions to the letter. It made complete sense; I reasoned that they were the experts and I was the recipient of their care, necessarily passive. So I listened dutifully to everything they had to say.

Often what they said was:

"You have to go see another specialist."

"I'll switch you to a different version of this drug – don't worry about the side effects."

"Let's run five more tests."

I followed their instructions without analyzing how it made me feel. I figured that more appointments, more pharmaceuticals, and more tests would be good for me; the more treatment I could throw at my disease, the better.

In the past I'd often compared my body to a car with irritating problems. I felt I had to keep driving it forward, or I'd be stranded on the side of a busy highway. If my "automobile" started to complain, I would step on the gas harder. I thought of my body as an aggravating "thing," an exasperating object separate from my true self.

Now the doctors were treating my body as a machine too, and looking at its many parts in isolation. When a problem cropped up, they offered suggestions as to how to fight it – but it was like playing a game of whack-a-mole: A tingling in my arm would develop, and I'd take something for the symptoms. But then a different sort of tingling in the other arm would crop up and it was back to the drawing board.

I kept throwing money at the disease. But as I rushed from one appointment to the next, trying to find a quick solution for this serious, long-term health issue, I did not feel much better at all.

With a sinking heart I noted that my balance and mobility were actually getting worse. I walked like the town drunk and was forced to use a cane my mother had given me – thank goodness it was collapsible. The side effects from my medication were staggering: I was awake half of the night and the drugs revved up my brain so much I was always on and babbled incessantly.

Even worse than these annoyances were the psychological effects of having a serious and unpredictable illness that my efforts were failing to control. I was always bumping into things and although I got back on my feet again, I felt like a failure.

Guilt began to dominate my life. I'd always struggled on the inside with low self-esteem, and my achievements at school and in business had served to conceal a deeply rooted inferiority complex. Now that I could no longer do what others did – walk in a straight line, run to catch a plane, give a top performance in the boardroom (or at least not consistently) – I felt worthless inside.

Just as I'd always wanted high grades and robust profit margins, I desperately wanted to check "bounced back from MS" off my to-do list and continue full speed ahead as normal. My body could not, would not, comply.

## Feeling Powerless Over an "Enemy"

My diagnosis had started a chain reaction in which I felt powerless. There was endless shuffling around between doctors: neurologists; physical therapists; psychiatrists; ear, nose, and throat specialists; and more. Months turned into years as I was shunted around between doctors. Sometimes I would feel optimistic when I'd had a couple of better days or even a week or two of modest improvements, but nothing seemed to work for me in the long term. I would get excited about a new treatment only to end up disappointed as no two days were ever the same. My suffering felt endless, and even though I am by nature a fighter, I was running out of hope.

Still, I kept looking for an answer outside of myself. For six long years I shuttled from one doctor to another and took many conventional medications. Often I thought to myself: *This new treatment regimen will finally make me feel at home in my body.* But it never seemed to happen.

Finally I capitulated to the aches and pains I felt on a daily basis; I didn't have the strength to rush around anymore as my energy level had plummeted. It was an effort just to figure out where my feet were and navigate from point A to point B. I stopped traveling and worked from home. On my very worst days I did not have enough energy to wash my face. When things reached crisis point, my doctor would arrange for me to be admitted to hospital for intravenous steroid treatment. This would sometimes bring about a short-term improvement.

Finally, Mike and I decided to close the business, and I resigned myself to a lifetime of fighting off symptoms as they came up. It felt as though my body were an enemy that had finally ground me down.

## My First Morning Pages – Left-Handed?!

It was March 1998 when I changed course and set off on my journaling journey for the very first time. I saw it as a physical therapy, but soon discovered it had dimensions I knew nothing about!

A month earlier I had suffered a hideous exacerbation of my MS. I had been in the kitchen cooking when I suddenly lost my grip on a pot of rice and it crashed to the floor. There was a catastrophic loss of sensation in my right side and it felt qualitatively different from previous flare-ups I'd had. Previous episodes when I'd lost sensation had lasted days, or weeks at most, but I felt sure this was different and might not go away anytime soon. So I started researching how I could adjust to this new feeling and keep functioning in spite of it.

Most irksomely, I was having difficulty writing. My right fingers shook; my right wrist buckled and ached. Not wanting to accept defeat, I started to research how I could teach myself to write with my left hand. My studies revealed many complicated methods, but I felt there must be a simpler way.

One weekend I had been feeling particularly determined to push through the obstacles my body had been putting in front of me. I had been researching alternative therapies that might help, and a friend had told me about Julia Cameron's book on creativity *The Artist's Way*. So that Monday morning, I woke up primed to start using one of Cameron's recommended tools, Morning Pages.

This involves writing three pages every morning, without fail. No ifs, ands, or buts, says Cameron: just write. Morning Pages are thoughts pouring out in a "stream of consciousness – you just write anything and everything that comes into your head." As Cameron says, it is not high art or "proper" writing – you just write three pages of *anything*, even if it's trivial in nature. This approach appealed to me; my main goal was physical therapy as I trained myself to form letters with my left hand, and I reasoned that it wasn't too important what I wrote about.

My alarm went off at 5:30 as usual. I showered and brewed a cup of black coffee. From a shelf above my desk I reached – with my left hand – for one of the plain yellow legal pads I'd bought in a ten-pack. I figured it would take me lots of practice to hone the ability to write legibly with my non-dominant hand. My pen of choice was black and clear stemmed.

Showered, caffeinated, and ready with pen and paper, I had everything I needed. I stared down at the paper and rested my right hand on the desk. The page looked back up at me, big and blank.

With my left hand, I picked up the pen. And even though my penmanship was not great, and I didn't have any big news to report, I put the pen to paper and let go. *Just write*, I told myself.

I don't remember what exactly I wrote about that morning. But I'll never forget how it made me feel. The struggle of learning to write with my non-dominant hand faded into the background as the words fell out of me. Suddenly, it felt natural to write. Sentences, paragraphs, and then pages flowed. Something inside me opened up as a profound connectedness to my body started to reveal itself.

In that first week, my pages took me many places. Kennywood, a Pittsburgh amusement park that I used to love, appeared in the pages – and so did the name of my first "boyfriend" from eighth grade (fittingly enough, Bob Page). I felt and heard rhymes, and wrote my first-ever poem!

Memories flooded my mind as I wrote, and I realized something more than physical therapy was going on. I had found a highway into my unconscious mind and was unlocking memories of events that had deeply affected me. I vividly recalled how the nuns who had taught me at school yelled at me for being two minutes late to pick up my younger brothers, and I remembered how shy and afraid the incident had made me feel for a long time.

Connecting with my feelings like this freaked me out to begin with. It was a shock to realize that the frightened, shamed child of my past was still living in my body, and that the powerful negative emotions I had repressed as a child still existed within me. However, I soon discovered that reconnecting to my long-buried emotions was an essential part of a healing process. I was experiencing genuine feelings that I had buried for years, and writing about them was cathartic.

So I kept at my Morning Pages – three sides a day, pen to paper – and soon discovered the incredible power of journaling as my health began to improve. As I will explain in later chapters, I had embarked on a healing journey that would transform my life in all of its dimensions – physical, psychological, emotional, and spiritual.

Seventeen years later I am still writing Morning Pages and reaping the health benefits. I have regained around seventy percent of the function in my right side, without taking any prescription drugs, and I have saved around $100,000 in health insurance premiums (again, I don't advocate this approach for everyone, but it has worked for me). I can write legibly with my right hand, so I do my morning pages ambidextrously these days. I am in touch with my emotions and living the happy, healthy life I want to live. It's my goal in this book to help YOU live a happier, healthier life too.

## Journaling Power Tips

Are you ready to start your own journaling adventure? I am excited to share my knowledge and experience to help you get the most from your journaling practice. Throughout this book, I will introduce you to tools and techniques to help you in this life-transforming process. I am confident that if you follow my suggestions you will experience many, if not all of the benefits that others have experienced. These benefits are real and can be measured scientifically, as you will see in Chapter 7.

Let's begin with Morning Pages, because they are the basic tool of any journaling practice and have amazing stress-busting properties. They clear the mind of mental clutter like nothing else.

As I mentioned before, the Pages are a daily pen-to-page exercise of "stream of consciousness" writing. You write anything – and everything – that comes into your head until you've filled up three pages of your notebook.

How does this help? I will explain the psychology of journaling later on, but for now, here's a summary of what happens:

In our daily lives we all experience ruminating thoughts that drag us down. We worry about personal problems and the multitude of things we need to do. Perhaps it's the performance review at work that worries us most, or it might be the messy house, the family member who is sick, or the mountain of bills that must be paid.

We are also affected on an unconscious level by past hurts and traumas, including things that happened a long time ago. We have unresolved emotional issues that simmer away below the surface of our conscious mind and distract and upset us. We have regrets about past mistakes and wrong beliefs about ourselves. All this "stuff" can be floating around in our heads at any time, creating a blockage of fear and stress that interferes with our wellbeing and creativity.

Therapeutic writing helps us deal with this mental garbage. As you write, you move it out of your head and onto the page, where it loses a lot of its power to harm you. This "brain dump" is good for your health and unblocks creativity. You don't need to worry about the *content* of your pages – it's the *process* that heals.

Writing down your story in Morning Pages taps into your natural desire to express yourself in an in-depth narrative. Posting something on Facebook is not enough to satisfy this deep need. Humans are hard-wired for storytelling and desire a creative release.

While talking therapy, so popular in Western society a generation ago, is declining, interest in both creative and therapeutic writing has been exploding. Writing provides a cost-effective and creative solution to inner conflict and doesn't carry the cultural stigma that some people associate with talking therapy. In addition, it offers the option of meeting other flesh-and-blood writers or journalers (for example, though local writing groups or websites like CreateWriteNow.com).

Whether or not you desire to be part of a community, Morning Pages can help to liberate you and meet this deep yearning for self-expression. It doesn't matter if you lack experience in writing. Morning Pages are not meant to be art, but rather are intended to unblock your creativity.

In Cameron's words: "There is no wrong way to do Morning Pages. These daily morning meanderings are not meant to be art. Or even writing… Pages are meant to be, simply, the act of moving the hand across the page and writing down whatever comes to mind. Nothing is too petty, too silly, too stupid, or too weird to be included…

"All that angry, whiny, petty stuff that you write down in the morning stands between you and your creativity. Worrying about the job, the laundry, the funny knock in the car, the weird look in your lover's eye – this stuff eddies through your subconscious and muddies the day. Get it on the page."

## Guidelines for Morning Pages

So now you can try Morning Pages for yourself.

Follow these simple steps to start a transformative journaling practice:

- Prepare yourself to write longhand in a notebook. It doesn't matter whether your journal is pretty or plain; just choose a notebook and pen that you feel comfortable with. Pen-to-paper journaling helps you to connect to your body and how you are feeling emotionally.

- Choose a time that fits your schedule. Early morning is best if you can manage it, but time of day is not the most essential feature of Morning Pages. The main thing is to do them *every day*, whenever it suits you.

- Find a quiet, comfortable, and private place to write, where you will not be interrupted by anyone.

- Start writing and keep going as fast as you can until you have filled three pages. If you are struggling to reach this goal, then write as much as you can in twenty or thirty minutes.

- For the desired therapeutic effect, aim to write for a minimum of twenty minutes a day.

- Whatever appears on the page when you start writing is fine. Often you will notice that you move from trivial stuff on to more important issues. But don't worry if your pages don't seem intelligent or insightful – they are still extremely beneficial. If you are struggling to get started with your writing, use some of the **Journaling Power prompts** at the end of this chapter.

- Ignore negative thoughts like "this is a waste of time," "this will never work," or "I am not a writer." That is the voice of your Inner Critic. You will learn more about dealing with him in the next chapter, but for now, just tell him to go play in traffic.

- Don't show anyone else your pages – it's important that you have the freedom to write anything you want without worrying about other people's reactions. Keep your pages somewhere private, or shred them if you want to.
- Repeat this process daily, introducing different techniques as you learn them later in the book.

Morning Pages seem simple, but they are deceptively powerful. They help you calm your mind, meditate, and ask questions about the greater world around you. You may or may not consider yourself to be a religious or spiritual person, but doing your pages every day pushes you to consider your beliefs and values on a deeper level.

Morning Pages can bring up strong emotions that are not always comfortable to experience, but in the long term they help you become your happiest and healthiest self. You will experience many personal revelations on your journaling journey!

You will grow emotionally and spiritually as you continue to write, day in and day out. The hardest part is getting started, but try to see the pages as part of your essential daily routine. Like cleaning your teeth, journaling helps to keep you healthy.

It may seem too good to be true that the simple act of writing can yield great benefits, but you'll never know unless you make the effort and try it for yourself. So for the moment, suspend your disbelief and adopt the famous Nike slogan: *Just do it!*

## Journaling Power Prompts

If you are struggling with your pages, you can use these prompts to kick-start your entries. Once you get going, just let it flow and write three sides or as much as you can manage about absolutely anything.

- How would you describe yourself to others?
- What are the three character traits that best describe you?
- What is your greatest talent?
- What is the most unique thing about you?
- Who or what inspires you?
- If you could have three wishes granted, what would they be?
- What are your spiritual beliefs and values? What do religion, faith, and spirituality mean to you?
- Write a list of your achievements and your positive attributes. What do your loved ones appreciate about you?
- What did you hope for when you were a child? What delighted you then, and what makes you happy now?

In the next chapter you'll learn how to overcome writer's block and deal with self-sabotage. You *can* journal your way to the happy, healthy life that you want to live!

#WriteON!

# Taming the Inner Critic

*As long as a man stands in his own way,*
*everything seems to be in his way.*

—Ralph Waldo Emerson

Worsening MS symptoms forced me to give up full-time work back in 1998, the same year I began writing Morning Pages. I had time on my hands and decided to de-clutter my house. I was determined to clear out all sorts of garbage, from the internal baggage I'd accumulated in my emotional life to the physical clutter of my external world. And it was during this process that I had a burning revelation.

After my father died, my mother had organized all the kids' letters, pictures, and cards into mahogany boxes engraved with each of our initials. Inside the one marked MM was my old diary, which I had always referred to as DD (Dear Diary). As I held this small blue book, complete with its tiny padlock, I remembered how, over the years, writing had helped me dump pain and agony, and deal with my existential struggles. DD had been a reliable friend, especially during rough or uncertain periods, and it had always helped me figure things out. It was a forerunner to my grown-up journals.

I sat down with my old confidante and it was just like old times, with me grumbling, moaning, and dumping questions: "What's to become of me? What am I to do with my life?" But instead of predictably sitting there taking my abuse, DD answered back: "Well, you could always write!"

"How? Details, please," I begged. So I wrote, and I wrote. And my journal entries pointed me to writing books and courses. I kept journaling and looking back at the written work I'd completed in the past – school essays, weekly newspaper reporting clips, and corporate training programs. "That's it!" I exclaimed to myself. "My new career will be my old love: writing." So I set up my office and progressed from "just journaling" to "real writing."

Then the fun began.

My new-job jitters were physically debilitating events. My throat tightened, and my stomach twisted around on itself. What was this all about? With no prior frame of reference in this matter, I did what I always did with conflict: I ran away. I didn't enter my office for weeks.

But I had to solve this mystery, and my Morning Pages led me to think, as I had so many times before, about my Inner Critic. I'd learned about this concept from Emily Hanlon's book *The Art of Fiction Writing*. Emily has written a lot about the Inner Critic, the critical inner voice that stifles our creativity and personal growth. It is a voice that torments creative people like artists and writers, telling them that they are wasting their time and that their work is useless (or something along those lines). We all have some version of the Inner Critic in our psyche—it's like a sub-personality within us, putting us down. My Inner Critic was giving me a bad case of writer's block, or page fright, as I like to call it!

Once I had identified that my Inner Critic was behind all the panic attacks, I knew I had to control him. (By the way, I refer to my Inner Critic as "him" and I've even given him a name – Mic. But some people think of their Inner Critic as a "she" or an "it – it doesn't really matter. The main thing is to know that it exists. In this book I will use the pronouns "he" and "it" interchangeably when discussing the concept of the Inner Critic.)

As I continued writing my Morning Pages, I had an insight into how to deal with this nasty bully. Of course! I needed to draw on my business consulting experience.

I thought about how I'd trained managers in redesigning their work life to achieve corporate profitability. I would talk to my Inner Critic as if he were one of my change-averse clients who excelled at maintaining the status quo. He couldn't be any worse than some of those difficult clients I'd had.

Could he?

I scheduled daily meetings with him. He yelled many abusive and condescending accusations at me:

"Writing is so foolish, spending so much time on yourself. What, you, a writer? You were successful in business; you can't have a creative writing career, too! Ha. Ha. Ha."

I listened for a time, and then I confronted him: I told him off and put him firmly in his place. I set boundaries on what he was allowed to contribute, explained my writing goals, outlined my performance expectations, and engaged him in rewriting his job description!

With the Inner Critic under control, I've been able to actualize my potential as a writer. My first paid assignment was a blog article on the effect of journaling on the management of multiple sclerosis. When I cashed my paycheck I was grinning. Making an impact through sharing my experiences felt remarkable. I may never have had the confidence to put my story "out there" like that had my journal not empowered me to blast through my limiting fears.

Today, when my Inner Critic attends daily writing appoint-ments, he knows his behavior must be positive, his criticism timely and constructive. Oh, he still tries his tricks, but I take no nonsense. And some days, we even clink a Chardonnay over his progress. My Inner Critic's defensiveness is down, his self-confidence is up, and he's learning that health and happiness just might be a reasonable alternative to tyranny and torture.

If I hadn't tamed my Inner Critic, I would have never gotten my writing career off the ground. And I would have never launched my second successful business, CreateWriteNow.com (I'll tell you more about that in Chapter 6). As the company's Chief Inspiration Officer I've seen many people transformed through journaling, and you'll read some of their stories later. But none of this would have happened if I'd allowed my Inner Critic free rein. He absolutely had to be tamed.

Through my daily journaling I learned to recognize my negative automatic thoughts – those well-worn and limiting "tapes" that play in your head, over and over, as they inhibit progress. We all have these negative thoughts from time to time. Journaling has helped me eliminate them.

My Inner Critic also shouted loudly when I decided to follow my dreams to become a singer: again I had to talk to him very firmly. My journal revealed how he had been empowered through the treatment I received as a child. The message I got from my parents and teachers was to keep quiet and be invisible; this did not help me to become a creative writer or singer. At school I was once sent away from chorus for allegedly being tone-deaf (though the problem was actually my shyness).

These rejections affected me deeply. As I grew up, I began to think of myself as "staccato," a musical term that meant "with each sound or note sharply detached or separated from the others." I didn't feel that I expressed myself in a way that flowed naturally, so I kept my mouth shut. I didn't speak out, let alone sing out. As I progressed through elementary school, high school, and college, I excelled at solitary tasks that did not require me to speak out loud. My Inner Critic told me to keep quiet and I obeyed his commands.

Journaling enabled me to break this pattern and cast aside the negative self-image I'd developed. Remarkably, I became a singer despite the many discouragements I'd suffered as a child. As you'll see in Chapter 5, the daily practice of journaling led me to take the first step in this once-scary direction – and then the next step and the next. With the help of my journal, I committed to the daily practice that learning to sing well entailed.

Of course, that meant listening to my voice (oh, yuck!). I taped all of my voice lessons and forced myself to pay attention. In time, I learned how to treat myself kindly and gently and discovered how relaxing, breathing, and drinking water not only made me a better singer, but a far less wrinkled one!

Now if I'm honest, it's taken years to tame my Inner Critic. It wasn't an overnight victory. But it's all happened through journaling. Through writing every day, I've learned to live in the present moment. I've cleared out the old messages that seemed to be stuck deep in the cells of my body. Managing my Inner Critic was a huge part of my journaling practice for many years and I continue to grapple with him on a regular basis.

As you start your journaling practice, don't let your Inner Critic get the better of you. In the next section I'll explain how the Inner Critic develops and how you can keep him under control.

## Journaling Power Tips

It's good to be aware of the Inner Critic right from the beginning of your journaling journey. Some people have more trouble than others with this interfering entity, but pretty much everyone will experience his voice some of the time.

Right now you could be thinking: "The whole journaling idea is probably a waste of time because I'm not really a writer," or "I doubt journaling will change my life: it seems a bit of a hippie thing to do." These thoughts create resistance to the whole process, and that's typical of the Inner Critic. As soon as you try something a little bit different, he goes off on a tirade.

So let's unmask him and put him in his place!

Psychotherapist and writer Dennis Palumbo defines the Inner Critic as "the persistent, sometimes harsh and almost always shaming 'voice' that belittles or invalidates your work."

It is, of course, part of you, a component of your psyche that manifests almost as a sub-personality of who you are. It's linked to your ability to make judgements, discern your likes and dislikes, and form opinions so that you can make decisions.

The Inner Critic developed as soon as you had language skills and could understand your parents' comments, particularly when they used the word "no" and rebuked you. You internalized these comments, and began to hear their "no" even when they were not physically present. If your parents were often critical, then your Inner Critic became a powerful negative voice in your head, forbidding certain thoughts and behaviors. If your parents were very positive and encouraging then you may have experienced it far less. But the Inner Critic isn't just a product of your family upbringing – teachers and other authority figures, and the wider society you grew up in, were all influential in its development.

## Society and the Inner Critic

For example, as girls grow up in Western Society they are bombarded with messages about how they should look, how they should dress, what they should buy, what type of work they should do, and what kind of person they should marry. There are so many "shoulds" based upon societal norms and values (and imposed upon both men and women) that we can end up trying to fit into a mold.

31

But here's the deal: this mold very rarely fits who we really are as an individual. We are conscious whenever we break away from the cultural norm and do something unique and creative, or when we find ourselves thinking or behaving differently than other people. On these occasions, we often hear the voice of the Inner Critic, trying to squash our adventurous spirit and urging us to conform to other people's expectations.

The Inner Critic is particularly keen on telling us what not to do, and when he speaks, he triggers negative emotions like fear and sometimes even self-hatred. Some people find that their Inner Critic jabbers away at them constantly, like a radio station playing in the background, and disturbs their peace of mind.

So as you begin your journaling, you need to learn how to control your Inner Critic. Be aware of what he's saying and question the truth of every statement he makes, because he often lies through his teeth! Indeed, much of what he says about you is blatantly false. The Inner Critic will steal your soul if you let him – but you don't have to submit to this psychic abuse! As you learn to resist his critical comments he will eventually bother you less and less. And as you begin to control the Inner Critic through journaling, you will start to feel better about yourself in other situations too.

## Positive Self-Talk

Many of my clients are ultra-busy, whether this involves balancing careers with children, caring for others, or advancing professionally at lightning speed (like I did during my consultant years). When they sit down to journal, they feel pangs of guilt for spending time on themselves, when they could be spending it on something else.

If that's you, learn to create time for yourself. Interrupt your negative self-talk and replace it with a neutral and encouraging inner voice. Say: "This is my own special time and I deserve it. Later on today I will do some useful things for other people. Right now I am exploring my true self and this is important for me." Write these encouraging comments to yourself down in your journal. In time, you will be comfortable journaling for a few minutes each day and will not fear "wasting time."

I find that writing quickly, in the stream-of-consciousness or free-writing style, really gives the message to your body, your mind, and your whole being that you are important. Writing physically fast is a great way to fling your Inner Critic to the wayside. Inner Critics like to protest that we're wasting time when we write, create, and self-express. Stream-of-consciousness writing is like a slap in the face to those pesky voices.

## Encourage Your Inner Coach

As a journaler, you also need to encourage your Inner Coach. As well as the Inner Critic, we have within us a Good (and Wise) Inner Voice that has our best interests at heart. It may be harder to hear this voice but it's there all the same: it's been with us since day one. The more you challenge your Inner Critic, the more you will be able to hear your Good Inner Voice. We just need to spend a lot of time with our journal to repair the damage we've done to ourselves listening to the wrong voice in the past. Then we can begin to live our truth.

We will never be able to eliminate the Inner Critic from our thought life entirely, nor is it desirable to do so.

Dennis Palumbo points out that this critical voice is a double-edged sword. He writes, "The same Inner Critic that judges our work so severely provides us with the ability to discern our likes and dislikes, to form opinions, to make decisions... We need a sense of judgement to navigate the world."

33

So there's no need to kill off your Inner Critic and hold a funeral – just give him some social-skills training and teach him to be more helpful. When he makes an uninvited appearance in your Morning Pages and chimes in with a snarky opinion, don't take it to heart! Correct him with a compassionate and loving affirmation of yourself and tell him of your plans to move forward in life. With practice you will become an expert at tuning him out and replacing him with a positive voice.

## Journaling Power Prompts

When you write Morning Pages, try scribbling them as fast as you can for a few days. Read them back and see if you can find any negativity in them. Read all of the pages you've written so far. Do you spot the voice of your Inner Critic anywhere? Many people find that he repeats himself endlessly with the same messages in a continuous loop. They vary from person to person, but the gist is often along these lines:

"You're not good enough. You don't deserve success or happiness. You're foolish pursuing your dreams." These negative statements are damaging. Even if you've never written them down before, they've been inside your head, dragging you down, and you've been listening to them for years.

It's time to rewrite the harmful words of your Inner Critic.

## Journaling Exercise #1

On a clean page, write down the negative messages you've been sending yourself. For example:

"You are a mediocre painter (or writer, singer, artist, entrepreneur, mother, etc.) and you will never be successful or achieve your goals."

Now take your Inner Critic's negative words and transform them into a message that will support, inspire, or comfort you instead. If you are an artist, you might write:

- I have an incredible eye for perspective
- The painting I gave Sarah for her birthday is her most prized possession, and she always receives compliments on it
- I have a natural talent and it brings joy to many people

If you are planning to start a business, you might write:

- I've always been a hard worker and I don't give up easily
- I have lots of experience in relevant areas of work
- I'm good at seeing the big picture
- I'm good with figures

And so on…

Keep going and write as many positive statements as you can. Remind yourself of these positive affirmations every day for the next week, and speak them out loud to yourself.

## Journaling Exercise #2

Answer this question: Do you want to write your way to better health? If you're reading this book, I trust that you do. There is no "I should"; there is only "I want to."

Even if you know you want to become healthier, you may not have thought about your reasons in much depth. So now, turn to a blank page and write this title:

*"I am journaling because I want to..."*

- Set your timer for ten minutes and start it running.

- In the form of a list, complete the sentence in as many ways as you can. Your reasons can be big or small, but they will be outcomes that will make you healthier and happier. Journaling will help you with these goals. Remember – and this is crucial –there must be no "shoulds" in your statements.

- Take five minutes to reflect on what you wrote. Pick out the three reasons that are most important to you. Circle them and number them in order of priority.

- Look at what you've just done. You've written down the goals that are important to you and determined the top three. When was the last time you had that kind of clarity about what you're after in life?

**In the next chapter you'll learn more about how to listen to your body and write your way to better health.**

**#WriteON!**

## Healing from the Inside Out

*All healing is first a healing of the heart.*
– Carl Townsend

Journaling profoundly changed the powerlessness I felt over my physical self. With doctors constantly poking and prodding me, as well as presenting new theories of how I could live with MS whenever the wind blew, I had to take responsibility for my own health.

So for the first time ever, I sat down to journal about how I was feeling – mentally, physically and emotionally: MS symptoms and all. I realized by the end of this session that I was not just describing what was going on – the act of journaling was in itself bringing about a change. I felt much better. This was a huge revelation to me. I had never viewed writing as therapy until that moment.

So writing about physical and psychological states became a daily practice. First I would describe a symptom – for example, feeling dizzy, or a lack of sensation in my right hand. I would detail how this was making me feel; perhaps there were knock-on effects I could perceive physically, such as wrist discomfort arising from not using my hand due to numbness. I would also check into how the symptoms were making me feel emotionally.

Sometimes I would "interview" my various body parts and have two-way discussions with them in my journals! This may sound a little strange, but it really helped me to get to know myself better.

My painful hip was a case in point. When I first started a dialogue with my hip, I talked to it angrily (like the Inner Critic). I yelled: "You are making me feel rotten; you are a major problem to me!" However, as I carried on writing, I realized I needed to be compassionate toward my hip. I began to talk kindly to it, as a nurturing parent would speak to a child. I asked it gently: "What is wrong? Tell me, and I promise I won't be cross."

I was amazed when I wrote down a reply from my painful hip. It told me quite clearly: "You've been running and running, and pushing and pushing, and you haven't given me any attention at all!"

As I continued journaling, I realized that the pain in my hip was telling me something about unresolved childhood emotions. My parents had given me little time and attention when I was growing up (the full story of my childhood will be told in Chapter 4) and this deep-rooted emotional wound was being manifested in my body.

I began to comprehend what I needed to do for myself: I had to give my inner child the time and attention I never received in my developmental years. As I made time for myself and allowed my inner child to be heard, the pain in my hip gradually disappeared.

I began to see that my body was not just a series of connected mechanical parts, nor was my body something that I owned like a possession: my body was who I am, the real me, and it was amazingly, miraculously intricate. It was intrinsically spiritual as well as physical. I found myself thinking like King David when he addressed the Creator God of the Universe in Psalm 139:

*I praise you because I am fearfully and wonderfully made; your works are wonderful,*

*I know that full well.*

*My frame was not hidden from you when I was made in the secret place, when I was woven together in the depths of the earth.*

*Your eyes saw my unformed body; all the days ordained for me were
written in your book before one of them came to be.*

## Tuning Into Myself

Through journaling I also discovered I was constantly beating
myself up for not being perfect. When I saw my thoughts written
down I realized the way I talked to myself was hypercritical and
abusive. I began to replace this harsh self-judgment with kind and
compassionate self-talk. I selected different words for my vocabulary
and I used a new, gentler tone of voice. I became a Nurturing Parent
rather than a Critical Parent (borrowing the terminology from
Transactional Analysis therapy).

For example, I used to think about my brother's genius at
playing the piano, and compare myself to him. I would tell myself:
"You are dumb and stupid, Mari." But I learned to treat myself
more compassionately. I recalled that I too had been a good piano
player, as well as a good student and a hard worker. So I learned to
encourage myself with gentle words:

"You have remarkable skills too, Mari. You are good with words
and creative thinking. You can own your strengths and talents."

I find it interesting that many people with MS have Type A,
self-critical personalities. The way their immune system attacks their
own bodies seems to mirror how they attack themselves internally
with harsh self-criticism. In view of this I have eliminated the need
to be perfect and made excellence my new goal. This new positive
approach has worked wonders for my self-esteem.

I have also benefited from becoming aware of my breathing
patterns. I discovered I was in a vicious cycle of shallow breathing,
which increased anxiety levels. When I began to breathe correctly I
stopped stressing myself out so much. I realized that I'd been stuffing

all of my emotions deep inside and so I began to express my emotional life in my journal. I began to take care of my heart.

I had to recognize that what I felt physically and emotionally mattered. Through the process of putting pen to paper, I acknowledged my current reality. I realized I should not gloss over my symptoms or ignore them. Health annoyances like mouth sores, sinus discomfort, and so forth, did not improve when I tried to shove them away and ignore their existence. Instead, the symptoms improved when I got in touch with them, owned them in my journal, and decided that I wanted to devote real time, effort, and energy to feeling appreciably better.

I'd ask my journal, "What's going on here?" and I'd write a few paragraphs describing what I was feeling and how that was affecting my day. Then, very naturally, I would plunge deeper (barely lifting my pen or pencil from the page). I would ask myself, "OK, what's *really* going on here?"

That practice of tuning in to my emotional state, the time it took to transmit thoughts to paper, the physical nature of wielding that pen (as my left-handed writing thankfully got better and better!), all combined to uncover truths about what I was feeling. Instead of drinking more black coffee to combat my fatigue, for instance, I learned to sit with the feeling, identify the trigger, and change my ways so that I felt refreshed.

So instead of reaching for more caffeine, I would just sit with the tiredness, breathe deeply, and acknowledge: "You are exhausted. Let's just explore what's going on." I would approach my issues from a heart perspective. I stopped reacting in a knee-jerk fashion and expecting instant solutions. I learned to live more in the present moment.

I began to see more clearly how physical states triggered emotions and how, conversely, emotions could create physical effects.

Now, I'm not saying that all physical maladies are caused by emotional conditions. To claim that would be to deny that medical pathologies, germs, bacteria, and parasites do exist. But physical health is so completely intertwined with emotional health that it's a wonder that so many of us deny the link.

Even though I'm widely considered to be an intelligent person, I never gave this connection a second thought until I started to journal and saw it all written down in black and white. My daily entries revealed how much impact my thoughts exerted on my physical self.

Writing helped me to recover a sense of identity that was fundamental to the healing process. I had been feeling like a victim for many years, but as I wrote, I felt I was regaining control over my life. I had a sense of being cleansed, of clearing out the emotional garbage I had accumulated in my life, and connecting to my spiritual self. And as I continued journaling, my energy levels began to improve. I had rediscovered my youthful passion for writing and decided I would give myself opportunities to develop my talent in this area.

So I went to Glastonbury in England for a writing retreat with Emily Hanlon. Emily had influenced my thinking and I was looking forward to meeting her face-to-face.

By the time I went to Glastonbury, my energy levels had increased significantly but I was still taking strong prescription medication. This drug had to be administered every week by injection and my trip meant I had to interrupt the treatment schedule. I didn't feel too worried about this and decided I would skip the injections completely while I was in Glastonbury. So for two weeks I took no prescription drugs and just did lots of writing. I was expressing my emotions a great deal and I was amazed at how much better I felt.

Wow, I feel so good, I told myself. It must be time to tell the doctor I don't want all these drugs anymore! So when I was back home I explained that conventional medical treatment was not working for me. It was not as if the drugs were a cure anyway; they were intended to manage symptoms, but they were not working for me. I was paying out $10,000 a year for medical insurance to cover ineffective treatment.

So I took a step of faith. I cancelled my insurance and started to look to alternative healthcare to meet my needs. I was extremely careful throughout this transition to tune into how I was feeling. I was a little nervous but wanted to give it a shot. It didn't make sense financially to be paying so much money for something I wasn't using. So I decided I would go to the emergency room if and when I needed it, and pay for healthcare only when it was necessary. This proved to be the right decision for me. I have not needed prescription drugs for the past decade and as I mentioned earlier, I've saved $100,000.

## My Own Primary Healthcare Provider

In 2001 I started taking full responsibility for my own health and wellbeing and I began to use doctors and other health professionals as resources I could tap into to help me improve the condition of my body and soul. I became my own Primary Healthcare Provider and I've gone from strength to strength.

It has been a gradual process of healing, involving all three dimensions of myself (body, mind, and spirit) as I've learned to care for myself holistically. Journal in hand, I am empowered to decide what I need in order to achieve wellbeing. I advocate for myself to receive the treatments that help me and I dump those that don't.

In this vital role, I set—and reach—many goals. I have restored my right side (as well as the rest of my body) to a higher level of healthy functionality. Thanks to this progress I now write my Morning Pages ambidextrously. The right side of my body is about seventy percent functional, and my right-handed writing is legible.

My journal and I are currently working toward the goal of retiring my walker. When I start a journaling session in the morning, I write a question like, "How do I walk from the bottom of my front porch steps to my car without my walker?" Then I reflect on that question by going into a meditation before journaling the answer. Sometimes I do some free writing, often with a .03 oz. bite of 88% dark chocolate. I talk to my journal and very often sing. I write a few phrases, sometimes put my iPod on shuffle, and see what the Universe wants me to hear. It all depends on my feelings (not what I think I should be doing). It depends on how the spirit moves me.

Journaling prompted me to change my diet to include fresh foods only, and I haven't used prescription drugs in eleven years or over-the-counter drugs in five. I haven't carried health insurance since I went off prescription drugs, as the healthcare practitioners I partner with (massage therapists, energy healers, and Reiki masters) are not covered under currently available healthcare policies. As I said before, this may not work for everyone, but it has worked for me and saved me a lot of money.

Every night, before I go to sleep, I religiously write my Night Notes. These are similar to Morning Pages and I'll explain more about how they work in Chapter 7. Writing Night Notes calms my mind; once I've written all my current concerns down on paper I don't need to worry about remembering them. This "mind-dump" enables me to sleep routinely through the night for seven to eight hours.

Most importantly, I no longer view my own body as an enemy. I do not fear what it will do. I know and love myself unconditionally and my relationship with my body is positive and compassionate. My journal has helped me listen to my body's needs much more effectively.

When I first started journaling, my journal let me know that I needed a long vacation, as I'd worked non-stop for eight years. And I heeded its advice and took a complete break from working. For weeks and weeks and weeks, I did nothing. I learned to love relaxation. And I used my fine-tuned left-brain (my business brain) to re-examine my priorities and revise my to-do lists.

## Asking My Journal

I used my free time to ask my journal lots of questions, digging deeper and deeper for the answers. Some days my entries bored me. Sometimes my brilliance baffled me.

Words, phrases, and sentences prompted me to ask myself, "Where did that comment come from?" "Who told me that?" "How did I ever think that?"

Some of my insights were quite staggering. For example, I discovered that MS was actually a gift from the Universe! My disease had forced me to live my life differently, and was giving me an opportunity to change what I'd been doing for almost forty years: emotionally and intellectually mistreating myself. With the help of my journal, I was getting to know the person who lives in my body.

Before that summer of reflection, I never thought much about my life. But once I had started to pay attention to myself, I began to understand and accept my strengths; I began entertaining my possibilities. I want to encourage you to do the same.

Your journal can speak to you too, and reveal the deep secrets of your heart. When you begin to follow your dreams and desires, you will find new opportunities begin to unfold. I believe that, just like me, you can journal your way to whole health.

## Journaling Power Tips

When I talk to the CreateWriteNow community I always say that there are no rules to follow with journaling. You create your own practice to suit your lifestyle, personality, and core values. However, there are two guiding principles I adhere to:

First: journaling should be done by putting pen or pencil to page and writing longhand. Second: I believe it should be part of a daily routine, whether during the morning, before bed, or both.

As a practice, journaling opens up new vistas, both internally and externally – and in this way, the practice is about freedom. But I advise all my clients to follow these two principles, and I follow them very strictly myself.

Pen-to-paper journaling solidifies the link between mind and body in many ways. It enables us to discover that we really live in our whole bodies, including our physical and figurative hearts, as well as in our heads. Many of us have learned to live in our heads at the expense of our hearts and bodies. Yet to be truly happy and healthy, and to discover our true destiny, we need to express all aspects of ourselves.

Putting pen to paper is a whole body experience. Think of it as an exercise, like walking three miles or riding your bike around the neighborhood. If you don't usually write longhand, you may get minor discomfort in your hands at first, but it will soon pass as your muscles adapt.

In today's world we are accustomed to banging things out very quickly, but there is value in the extra time it takes to journal in longhand. Journaling by hand makes us more aware of what is going on inside us physically, from head to toe. We can tune into what is troubling us and there is enough time to work things through and find solutions as we write. As we see how consistently this process works, we realize we are in control and are empowered.

If you adopt a daily, pen-to-paper approach, you will immediately benefit and start to see personal growth and effective solutions to your challenges. Circumstances don't always change immediately, but as your attitudes improve and you learn to challenge your own negative self-talk, you will feel better and see positive gains in many areas.

Journaling will help you to become your own Primary Healthcare Provider too, if you wish. You can learn how to be responsible for your own wellbeing and select the resources that will help you to improve your health and live a happier life. You may be a little fearful of this, as society encourages us to rely on doctors all of the time. But you can make positive lifestyle choices and learn to heal yourself.

*Trust yourself.*

There is a deep wisdom available through journaling. Depending on your own background and beliefs, you may view this power as something within yourself (a Higher Self) or you may see this wisdom as coming from God, a Higher Power, or the Universe. As you progress with your journaling, you will learn to listen to this voice of wisdom that knows what is best for you and your life. And you will learn to reject the negative voice of the Inner Critic.

The next section focuses on listening to your whole self: body, soul, and spirit. Respond to the prompts and write down anything that comes into your mind, without censoring yourself.

## Journaling Power Prompts

Before you do these exercises, check that you are breathing properly.

Breathing is something you take for granted. It's such a basic necessity that there's no wrong way to do it, right? Well, not so fast. You may be taking shallower breaths than your body needs and not delivering a full dose of oxygenated air every time you inhale.

According to Harvard Health Publications, we often skimp on deep abdominal breathing because of cultural pressure to stifle strong emotions like anger or sadness. We also "suck in" our stomachs for a super svelte waistline – this is bad for our breathing too! When you resort to "chest breathing" instead of abdominal breathing, the small blood vessels in your lower lungs may not receive enough oxygen, making you feel short of breath and anxious. Deep breathing, on the other hand, slows the heart rate and can lower or stabilize blood pressure, leaving you feeling more relaxed.

## Journaling Exercise #1

So take a few deep breaths and relax your body. Ask yourself the following questions about your wellness right now, and write your answers in your journal.

- What three words would you use to describe your physical state at this moment? Your mental state? Which parts of your body feel good? Which hold pain or tension?

- What is your energy level on a scale of 1 to 10?

- Are you feeling tired or stressed? If yes, can you pinpoint the reason why? Do you often feel this way?

- Would you say that you feel well cared-for overall? Why or why not?

- How would you describe your relationships with friends, family, and co-workers right now? Are they healthy relationships? Are any of them causing you stress or pain?

Reread your answers. Does anything surprise you? Where do you see room for more health and healing in your life?

## Journaling Exercise #2

- Simply sit and be present for a few minutes. Take deep breaths and concentrate on each area of your body – one at a time. Ask yourself what the different parts of your body are feeling or trying to communicate. Which areas need the most attention?

- Write a letter from the perspective of your body. Share where you are experiencing stress, discomfort, or unease. Share where you feel strong and rested. How could you make changes or improvements in your day-to-day-habits?

## Mindful Eating

The food you eat every day has the power to heal or the power to harm. Take a closer look at what and how you eat. What foods nourish your body and leave you feeling strong and energized? Which foods do the opposite? Journaling about your food preferences, habits, and patterns can help you be more mindful in your decisions.

## Journaling Exercise #3

Describe your relationship with food, using these questions as a guide:

- Would you describe yourself as someone who lives to eat or eats to live? Do you enjoy shopping for and cooking food at home? What do you like to prepare?

- Do you like going out to eat? What kinds of dishes and flavors are you drawn to? What are your favorite foods? Do you have an emotional attachment or history associated with any of them?

- What feelings do you associate with eating? Are they generally positive (enjoyment, nourishment, comfort) or negative (guilt, shame, regret)? Why? Do you have any past medical or emotional problems associated with food?

- Write about a recent situation in which you made mindful and healthy eating decisions. Where were you? What time of day was it? How were you feeling? Who were you with? What did you eat and over what period of time? How did you feel after you finished your meal? What about this experience could you replicate in the future?

## Giving Thanks

When was the last time you stopped to count your blessings? Giving thanks doesn't have to be a once-a-year affair, and expressing gratitude frequently can help you be happier and healthier. Research shows that thanksgiving is consistently associated with positive emotions, improving health, appreciating good experiences, dealing with challenges, and building strong relationships. Now that's something to be grateful for.

## Journaling Exercise #4

- Free-write about things and people in your life that you are thankful for. Describe why you feel lucky to have them in your life.

- Now focus on what you are thankful for, specifically about your health. What might you be taking for granted – like having mobility or being pain free? What are you grateful to be able to do in your day-to-day life because of your health status?

- Write a short personal statement of gratitude.

## Spiritual Growth

Your spiritual health is an important part of your overall wellbeing. Spirituality has many different meanings, but it requires you to explore questions that don't have easy answers. For some, spirituality is developing a strong religious faith. For others, it is finding peace and purpose through yoga or nature or service to others. Explore your spiritual side and push yourself to explore and discover beyond your individual experience.

## Journaling Exercise #5

- Free-write about your current spiritual or religious life. Check in on what you believe and what you value.

- Dig deeper into some of the more challenging spiritual questions, including: What do you value most in life? • Do you feel you have a purpose? • Do you believe in God or a higher power? • What do you think is the most important part of leading a good life? • What do you think happens when you die? • Do you feel part of a community – whether that is small and local or large and global? • How do you pray, reflect, or meditate? • What gives you hope or comfort in difficult times? • What do you fear most? • What brings you joy? • Which people do you feel most connected to?

## Personal Philosophy

In your Morning Pages, you can continue to explore other aspects of health, such as physical activity, a good sleep pattern, and giving yourself enough leisure time. For each of these areas, ask yourself questions as you did in the above exercises.

After you have explored every aspect of your health, put your personal health philosophy into words. Craft a short mantra or a detailed mission statement – whatever helps you articulate your priorities and values. Meditate on this as you go forward in your journaling journey.

**In the next chapter, we'll look at how past experiences affect us and how we can deal with painful memories through journaling.**

#WriteON!

# Rewriting History

*Life can only be understood backwards;*
*but it must be lived forwards.*

—Soren Kierkegaard

So many people (myself included) have been fearful about life. We can be comfortable living with fear: it fits snugly, and we can't imagine anything different. For instance, we might worry that if we take a moment for ourselves without thinking about work, we will fall off the ladder to success and everything we've worked so hard for will come crashing down.

Sometimes, taking the time to write and listen to our bodies feels much more risky than simply pushing our emotions to one side. It seems easier just to ignore our nagging physical pains, like indigestion or headaches. But often these symptoms are rooted in past hurtful experiences and the repressed emotions that we carry in our bodies. Traumatic events in childhood can have long-lasting repercussions.

Journaling about past experiences can be difficult, as we work through painful emotions. The process can bring up memories that are far from pleasant. But in the long run, exploring these emotive events through writing is cathartic. Acknowledging our past removes its power to hurt and control us. So we can give ourselves permission to feel these hurts, and tolerate the short-term pain as part of a healing process.

Personally, I've confronted some very painful memories from childhood; as I journaled I remembered how the adult caregivers I relied on did not always give me the best of care.

I realized how much responsibility I carried as a child within my family. I was the eldest of four children all born within a period of five years. My parents married when my mom was 33 years old (at a time when mothers in their thirties were considered elderly). Mom and Dad wanted to complete their family before Mom reached the taboo age of 40, and that's why we were born so close together. As Mom was under pressure, I was encouraged to become "Mommy's little helper" and was always looking after my younger siblings.

Through journaling, I recalled how I was treated differently from my brothers and sister, and seen as part of the grown-up team. I was given special privileges, and extra responsibility. There was an upside and a downside to this special treatment. I was often allowed to dine with Mom and Dad, if they had something special to eat, which made me feel grown-up. However, from quite early on in childhood, I felt like a parent. I developed a huge sense that it was my duty to take care of other people.

My father took me everywhere with him, whether he was going to the shops, to church, or to get his hair cut. I was treated much like an eldest son, and looking back, I don't think I really had a childhood. To my dad, I was not a person in my own right. This was partly a cultural thing, related to growing up the 1950s, when society was less child-centered. In those days many parents showed little emotion and children were expected to keep quiet.

Although my father loved me, he was unable to demonstrate any real feeling – and so I was unable to experience his love. I also learned from Daddy Dearest (that was my pet name for my father) how to repress all my emotions. This was not a good legacy. Later on in life

I felt much like a robot at times, functioning well intellectually, but feeling nothing inside.

My journal also revealed the damage caused to my sensitive inner child by my educational experiences in Catholic grade school. Sometimes the nuns who taught me shouted at me, and failed to acknowledge my sensitivity. The harsh treatment I received left painful scars. It was part of an institutionalized form of religion that left me feeling stupid and shameful, as if I was "not good enough." It didn't help with my self-image that I was left-handed, and forced by the nuns to write with my right hand because "the left hand is the devil's workshop." As a consequence my writing was too big and I was further criticized.

There was little taught in grade school about the love and grace of Christ in the New Testament; it all seemed to focus on the Old Testament and the Ten Commandments. The nuns' emphasis on religious law intensified the guilt that haunted both my childhood and adult life.

Looking back now, I have worked through my anger and see that the nuns had not been trained to understand child psychology; I have forgiven them for wounding my inner child. I am pleased that the current pontiff, Pope Francis, seems to represent a more compassionate form of Catholicism than the one I grew up with.

As I've explored my childhood through my journal, I've gained a sense of perspective that has brought me peace. There is no doubt I was deprived of affection, but I have allowed myself to feel the pain, and move on to the point of forgiveness. I can now acknowledge there were also positives in my earlier years. My parents felt it was their job to care for me practically – feed me, clothe me, and help me to get a good education and make something of my life. They were wonderful in all of those things, and took us on lovely vacations too; they just didn't do emotion.

Through my journaling journey, I've found increasing freedom from the effects of childhood trauma. I have learned how to put my past where it belongs: behind me. Journaling compelled me to admit that I had wounds that were still open, but it also revealed how I could heal them and move forward. It showed me that I had the power, intelligence, and talents to change my thoughts and behaviors.

## Journaling Power Tips

Most of us carry around memories that we would rather forget, but writing them down brings perspective. We realize that we cannot change the past. Some of my clients have remembered their parents being alcoholics, or withholding expressions of love. But they continued to journal and work through their painful feelings. Today they feel emotionally free and able to declare: *That was me thirty years ago. But that's not me now.*

To get to the juicy part of living in the present, we have to confront our baggage. But when we have dealt with our memories, we can say: *OK, that's the past, that's what happened, but it was not my fault that my parents divorced* (for example). We become aware of situations that trigger our old issues and gain the tools to deal with them. We catch ourselves whenever we resort to old, destructive patterns and stop ourselves, thinking: *I'm responding the same way I always did; what's that all about? Time for more journaling.*

Through journaling, knowledge becomes power. With knowledge, we can change the old tapes that play in our heads. Sometimes we have to commit extra time to writing about particularly difficult issues. And that's what I tell people over and over. But the end result, emotional freedom and self-knowledge, is worth the effort it takes.

Journaling is recommended as a tool for healing by Donna Jackson Nakazawa, author of *Childhood Disrupted: How Your Biography Becomes Your Biology, and How You Can Heal.* As you may know,

Nakazawa is a science journalist of high repute. In her book she explores the lifelong consequences – both emotional and physical – of Adverse Childhood Experiences (ACEs). She looks at the long-term effects of early stressors, such as being abused or neglected; losing a parent; living in a dysfunctional or very poor family; witnessing parents going through a divorce or living with a severely depressed parent (this is not an exhaustive list). She argues that ACEs shape our biology and seriously affect our physical and emotional resilience as adults.

Early traumas can predispose us toward chronic illnesses like heart disease, cancer, auto-immune disease, fibromyalgia, chronic fatigue syndrome, and depression, says Nakazawa. She presents compelling evidence that many serious health conditions are linked to stressful events in childhood. She herself has suffered from several life-limiting auto-immune illnesses, including Guillain-Barré syndrome. She was emotionally devastated as a child when her father, whom she adored, died suddenly: she believes this triggered her auto-immune problems.

Nakazawa outlines how chronic adversity can change the archi-tecture of a child's brain, altering the expression of genes that control stress hormone output. She believes the resulting hormonal changes initiate an over-active inflammatory stress response that persists for life. So childhood adversity potentially damages us on a cellular level. Adults who have experienced ACEs show a greater erosion of telomeres – the protective caps that sit on the end of our DNA to keep it healthy. And time alone does not heal all of this early damage.

"Your emotional biography becomes your physical biology and together they write much of the script for how you will live your life," says Nakazawa.

Her suggestion is to "re-boot" the brain and create new healthy neural pathways using a mindfulness-based stress reduction program.

This involves disciplines like meditation and yoga, along with dietary and other lifestyle improvements – and very importantly, *therapeutic writing.*

She urges people to express their painful stories in a journal. "Even if you have no health-care practitioner to share your story with, you can begin to speak your truth by 'writing to heal,'" she says. "This creates the experience of seeing yourself for who you really are, perhaps for the first time in your life."

It is my personal experience that writing about my childhood and adolescence has improved my health and wellbeing. If you feel that you had a hard time as a child or young person, I urge you to write about it. Writing about a traumatic experience will make you feel sad in the short-term, but the sadness is usually short-lived, a matter of a few hours. And many scientific studies suggest that in the long-term you will benefit.

James Pennebaker, the pioneer of expressive writing research, states in *Expressive Writing: Words That Heal*: "Writing may make you sad for a brief time, but the long-term effects are far more positive. Across multiple studies, people who engage in expressive writing report feeling happier and less negative than they felt before writing…. Reports of depressive symptoms, rumination and general anxiety tend to drop in the weeks and months after writing about emotional upheavals…and studies show improvement in overall wellbeing and improved cognitive function."

So it's worth facing up to long-repressed emotions and allowing yourself to experience them, because in the long-term, expressive writing has a healing effect.

## Journaling is a two-way process

To fully harness the power of journaling, it is important to understand that the practice is like a two-way street. It's not just dumping and dumping and dumping (although it can be seriously useful for that). It's a learning process, too. You'll become aware of your deepest motivations and beliefs. Some of these beliefs may be worth hanging on to – others will be outdated and will limit the person you want to be. Challenge those beliefs and adopt new ones! Cultivate self-knowledge, but remember self-compassion too.

Don't forget to look out for the Inner Critic and keep him firmly in his place. As you explore your early experiences, you may see how the Inner Critic developed in your life through the judgments and comments of other people. You don't have to accept other people's declarations over your life, so challenge these erroneous beliefs that were imposed on you long ago. Just because someone told you were awkward or stupid (or any other unjustified description) you don't have to believe it for the rest of your life. You owe it to yourself to cast off all the labels that others have given you, and re-define yourself in your own terms.

When you look back at the past, you will probably feel angry with the people who have hurt you – and you may be mad at yourself too for some of the mistakes you've made! Make a decision to forgive yourself, and work toward forgiving others too. Letting go of anger and resentment is good for you – physically, emotionally and spiritually. If you've been abused, forgiving an abuser is difficult, but it is definitely possible. You don't have to condone what was done to you or have any contact with the person who has hurt you. However, you need to recognize that holding on to the pain is very bad for your health. Your anger usually has no effect on the person you are angry with, but it causes dis-ease within your body and soul. It's not worth holding on to toxic emotions: you have a choice, so choose emotional freedom!

## Journaling Power Prompts

## Journaling Exercise #1

It may help you to understand your childhood if you complete the ACE questionnaire below from the website www.acestudy.org (where you can find more information on this ongoing collaborative study between the Centers for Disease Control and Prevention in Atlanta, GA, and Kaiser Permanente in San Diego, CA).

This is the official ACE survey and it assesses the number of Adverse Childhood Experiences you had. For each question, circle Yes or No and add up your score when you've answered all of the questions.

<u>Finding Your ACE Score</u>

While you were growing up, during your first 18 years of life:

1. Did a parent or other adult in the household often or very often... Swear at you, insult you, put you down, or humiliate you? or Act in a way that made you afraid that you might be physically hurt? Yes No If yes enter 1 _____

2. Did a parent or other adult in the household often or very often... Push, grab, slap, or throw something at you? or Ever hit you so hard that you had marks or were injured? Yes No If yes enter 1 _____

3. Did an adult or person at least 5 years older than you ever... Touch or fondle you or have you touch their body in a sexual way? or Attempt or actually have oral, anal, or vaginal intercourse with you? Yes No If yes enter 1 _____

4. Did you often or very often feel that... No one in your family loved you or thought you were important or special? or Your family didn't look out for each other,

feel close to each other, or support each other?
Yes No If yes enter 1 _____

5. Did you often or very often feel that... You didn't have enough to eat, had to wear dirty clothes, and had no one to protect you? or Your parents were too drunk or high to take care of you or take you to the doctor if you needed it?
Yes No If yes enter 1 _____

6. Were your parents ever separated or divorced?
Yes No If yes enter 1 _____

7. Was your mother or stepmother: Often or very often pushed, grabbed, slapped, or had something thrown at her? or Sometimes, often, or very often kicked, bitten, hit with a fist, or hit with something hard? or Ever repeatedly hit at least a few minutes or threatened with a gun or knife?
Yes No If yes enter 1 _____

8. Did you live with anyone who was a problem drinker or alcoholic or who used street drugs?
Yes No If yes enter 1 _____

9. Was a household member depressed or mentally ill, or did a household member attempt suicide?
Yes No If yes enter 1 _____

10. Did a household member go to prison?
Yes No If yes enter 1 _____

Now add up your "Yes" answers: _____ This is your ACE Score.

For every question where you scored a point, write about your adverse childhood experience. (A word of warning here: if you have suffered extreme abuse, please consult a mental health professional before doing this exercise; you may need to do it in a supported environment). If you become very distressed during any writing exercise, stop writing and seek support.

It's worth noting that the ACE questionnaire does not cover every type of emotional trauma suffered in childhood. You may have been through a difficult time when the adults around you either hurt you or failed to support you, and that particular experience is not included in the survey. It is not easy to quantify every source of emotional pain. Even if you did not tick any boxes, you may still carry scars.

Less visible forms of suffering might include the following:

- Growing up in poverty (or in poorer circumstances than your peers)

- Being forced to take on too many chores or adult responsibilities at an early age

- Living with a highly manipulative or critical parent or guardian

- Being bullied at school or elsewhere (intensely or over a long period)

- Being part of a minority ethnic or religious group and encountering prejudice within the wider community

- Being chronically ill and having to spend a lot of time in hospital or undergoing invasive medical procedures

- Being exposed to pornography or graphic horror movies

- Living in an unhappy and emotionally intense environment

If any of the above apply, or a situation comes to mind, take the time to journal about what happened and unpack your feelings.

When you have completed the above exercise, use the prompts below:

- How did you feel after writing about your childhood?
- What are your happiest memories as a child or young person?
- Can you find any positives in the situations you wrote about?
- Is there anyone you need to forgive?

## Journaling Exercise #2

Before you begin, bring to mind a situation where someone treated you badly. Write about how you felt before, during, and after this event took place. Write about your deepest feelings.

Now focus your attention on the person responsible for hurting you and write about the incident from his or her perspective. Why do you think they did what they did? What led up to the event, and were there mitigating circumstances?

Do you feel you can forgive this person, now or perhaps gradually as you come to terms with your memories?

## Journaling Exercise #3

This exercise is called "the Unsent Letter."

Write a letter to the person who has hurt you. Describe the events that happened and tell them exactly how you felt when they treated you badly. Don't hold back; write everything down.

Finally, if you feel you can forgive them, end your letter with a declaration of forgiveness. (Remember that the person who benefits most from your forgiveness is you.)

Now tear the letter up, or burn it! As you destroy the letter, let go of your hurt and angry feelings. If you have a spiritual perspective on life, you can pray a prayer of blessing over the person you have now forgiven. Speak the name of the person out loud and repeat "I forgive you and release you" three times. This is a powerful exercise, so repeat it for every person you know has caused you significant hurt.

Healing childhood memories is an important step in becoming a healthy, emotionally free individual. It helps you regain the confidence to be your true, authentic self.

#WriteON!

# High Notes and Harmony

*What lies before us and what lies behind us are small matters
compared to what lies within us. And when we
bring what is within out into the world, miracles happen.*

– Henry Stanley Haskins

Ten years ago, I was working in my journal on wanting to become a more vocal person. I had always been quiet and shy; when I did speak, it was physically painful, and I felt I was stupid. Usually I felt invisible. I had gone inside myself at an early age and had been living there ever since; speaking up was a physically painful experience, so it was much easier to just shut up.

Music, however, had been part of my life since childhood. I had always loved listening to it; I'd sit in my room, ears glued to my red-speckled phonograph or the radio. As I journaled, I recalled these musical memories, and as my pen hit the page, I felt them resonate from head to toe.

My mom introduced me to music at an early age. I loved listening to my earphoned transistor radio every night in bed to discover what stations and new music I could pull in.

I kept journaling, and recalled how I started taking piano lessons in 1958, the year Van Cliburn won the Tchaikovsky International Piano Competition. With my parents, I had watched that competition on TV, spellbound as his hands flew over the keys as if by magic. I decided I wanted to take part in that magic, too. So my parents enlisted some of the nuns who taught at school to teach my two younger brothers, my sister, and me in the afternoons, after classes ended. My lessons were held once a week.

One of my brothers, Stephen, had an incredible knack for the instrument; he didn't even need sheet music. He'd race through all the pieces that I, his older sister, was practicing diligently for many hours. It didn't seem to require much effort on his part. Meanwhile, my practice sessions were not exactly producing the kind of magic I'd seen during that famous international competition. At the age of nine I performed in the Pittsburgh Pianorama competition myself. But even though I placed in the top ten, I felt inferior.

It didn't help that my brother's playing had so impressed the nuns who taught us after school. Looking back, I realized that most of the nuns' star students were boys. Boys, at least, were the ones they lavished with praise.

About three years later, I gave up the piano. Practicing took too much time, and my parents didn't really encourage the pursuit. As a shy little girl, I felt intimidated by the nuns, and by my brother's outstanding talent. Stephen, however, continued to take the lessons every week and was showered with praise at home and at school.

My mother was a big music person, too, an avid singer. She would sing songs from the Great American Songbook around the house. I'd be sitting in the living room and hear confident strains of songs by Cole Porter, George Gershwin, and Frank Sinatra coming from the kitchen where she was setting the table. But when I tried to join in, I had the sense that I wasn't doing too well. My voice was off-key. How I longed to sound like my mother!

When I was ten, I tried to join my school chorus, the Choraleers. But after I sang five or six bars, the director told me bluntly that I was tone-deaf.

What was tone deafness, I wondered? Was it a disease? Did I need a doctor? Of course, good little fifth graders weren't supposed to ask for explanations or reasons why. And I didn't get any advice on how to prepare for another audition. (I mean, teachers are supposed to help kids learn, right?)

"I wish I could sing," I lamented to my mother.

"Honey, I wish you could, too," she said, confirming my worst fears. I never really tried again after that. Singing, I thought, was not my thing. So my severely shy ten-year-old self only performed bedtime duets in secret with her Jewel maroon transistor radio.

Talking wasn't really my thing, either. I wasn't vocal. Although I worked hard on my homework and studied carefully, I rarely raised my hand or spoke during class. I assumed no one really wanted to hear my voice. I focused instead on making sure my siblings were taken care of, and I let them shine.

Being a businesswoman reinforced my aversion to talking. As my business thrived, I excelled at writing reports, preparing bullet points, and that kind of thing. I never really spoke. I was not as dramatic as Maya Angelou, who literally did not speak for six or seven years, but I avoided speaking whenever I could. I shoved my thoughts and feelings away deep inside.

With most people I was quiet and shy, but, even worse, some people assumed I was stupid. As I wrote I realized how much my silence had harmed my self-image. The damage was still with me, even though I was over fifty years old. This realization made me more determined than ever to keep exploring my voice.

Somewhere in the course of journaling about my relationship to music and to my own voice, I wrote: "I will take voice lessons." I knew I was a hard worker and felt that with the right teacher, I'd learn to sing. And so it goes in my journaling journey: when I set my goals, the Universe provides avenues and options.

Soon after, I was leafing through a local newspaper when I saw an article about a place called Kingston Music School. The school was inviting "children of all ages" to enroll in its musical classes.

Because I'd been journaling about my physical voice and wanting to use it more freely, I zeroed in on what would make me happy and did not question it as I normally might have done. I reached for the phone, dialed, and told the receptionist I wanted to learn to sing. The strong, confident voice in which I said the words surprised me at first.

At the music school, I found some familiar faces. They were my Inner Critics, equal-opportunity creativity-destroyers! Fortunately, having encountered their tricks in my journaling journey, I had the skills to deal with them. My plan of action was to sing every day. I did not enjoy hearing my own voice to begin with, but I recorded my lessons and forced myself to pay attention. I dismissed the Inner Critics and spoke to myself kindly.

The director of the music school was probably in her early seventies. After her parents died, she had gone back to school and gotten a music degree. Her first career had been in biology, because both of her parents had been biologists. Fiercely determined to follow her passion, she reminded me of someone you would see in a movie. At times, she also reminded me of the nuns at school, but this time her strictness didn't daunt me.

I would not have taken those first steps or faced down my Inner Critics (and that strict teacher), if not for my transformative journaling journey. As I kept treating myself with compassion, I saw my dream of musical magic – no longer a pipe dream – come together harmoniously. Through it all, I kept writing.

One spring, about a year into my singing-lessons journey, I took part in a recital. It was at a middle school in Kingston, Massachusetts, the next town over from mine. In the auditorium were about one hundred and fifty audience members, as well as the most gorgeous baby grand piano I'd ever seen.

I was to perform with the other students at the music school, of which there were about twenty. They included a gentleman that played the violin and another young lady who was a singer, but otherwise, the other students were mostly kids: I was definitely the oldest "child" there.

During the dress rehearsal, I experienced the unfamiliar sensation of being onstage. It suddenly hit me: very soon I'd be singing up there, in front of everyone. Instead of the terror my intensely shy childhood self would have felt, I felt like I was in heaven. When the day arrived and I went onstage, the experience was sublime. I felt I was "out there" in the Universe, and it was the most natural feeling ever. I sang Frank Sinatra's "All The Way," echoing the refrains my mother used to sing in the kitchen. It had become my favorite Sinatra song, too.

After the crowd had filed out, my teacher asked, "How did it go? Were you scared?"

"No way," I answered, "When's the next recital?"

My mother passed away before I began this musical journey; but in my head, I like to continue our repartee about my singing. I imagine telling her, "Mom, I know I can sing," and she responds, "Oh, honey, I know you can, too."

## Music as therapy

In 2005 I decided I would like to record a song, and contacted Perry Rossi, whose state-of-the-art production studio is only ten miles away from my home. A technical maestro, Perry has been performing from the age of four, and I've learned so much from him in the past ten years. He has his own orchestra and an extremely high energy level, and is always performing live.

As soon as I walked into Perry's control room and heard my voice, I realized I was a real singer. I knew I'd only been singing for a couple of years, and had so much to learn, especially about the social and emotional aspects of singing, but I knew it would happen.

Being a great singer is all about expressing emotion, and Perry taught me to put myself into the song, to use crescendos and make the song my own, instead of simply fitting lyrics to notes. This really fell into place when Perry and I were working on my album *A Baby Boomer's Christmas* back in 2007, and I was recording Stevie Wonder's *Some Day at Christmas*. I love this sixties song with its message of love and peace. Perry explained I could adapt the timing and start late – I could make the song my own, just as Stevie Wonder had. Perry showed me the possibilities, and I found I could feel the story for myself. So I can truly say it was Perry who introduced me to my favorite four-letter word: *FEEL*.

While all of this was going on, and I was launching my recording career, the director of the Kingston School of Music decided to close the school. I talked to my journal about it and decided to look for a "holistic" voice teacher. My acupuncturist introduced me to Lisa Sheldon, who focused on getting me out of my head (memorizing notes and lyrics) and into my body. She showed me how to breathe properly, relax, and produce sounds without thinking about it. I was with Lisa for six years and she helped me to become an embodied singer.

In 2013 I felt – thanks again to my journal – it was time to move on. One day on Facebook, I saw a video and knew Justin Stoney was to be my new voice teacher. The Eastern proverb had proved true for me: *When the student is ready, the teacher will appear.* Justin's approach is revolutionary, and I was somatically ready to meet him.

As Justin lives and works in New York (he runs New York Vocal Coaching), I no longer drive to a local musical school where I'm the oldest "kid," and I don't perform in an auditorium: this new experience is unfolding through Skype. Justin's approach harmonizes with my pen-to-paper journaling, bringing transformation to my body.

In my last lesson I told him: "These days, I am really enjoying hearing myself talk and hearing myself sing." For me, this is profound healing.

During these lessons with Justin, I feel tuned in to a sense of spirituality, energy, and life force. Through my journaling and my work with Justin, my shoulders are now level. I have feeling on the right side of my body; progress indeed!

My singing lessons have shown me that I do have emotions – I am not the robot I used to think I was. Feeling the pitch and letting it rip takes me to new and exciting places in my own getting-healthier-by-the-day body. The holistic approach I've taken to my singing has helped to inform my writing.

Music is therapy to me, just as journaling is therapy. And I do believe more and more people will come to see that journaling is a holistic therapy with clinically proven benefits.

## Journaling Power Tips

You can see from my story how journaling reveals our deepest desires and helps us, step by step, to fulfill those dreams. I want to encourage you to continue your daily journaling and commit yourself fully to this long-term process. You will not arrive at your destination overnight, but I am confident you will get there, one day at a time.

The journaling process was crucial in releasing my creativity and gave me freedom to express myself through pen and paper. Then I learned to express myself vocally and it was wonderfully liberating. For me, music is one of my greatest inspirations in life. Becoming a singer was a major life goal and important to my identity and wellbeing.

Explore your authentic voice with your journal. It may or may not involve music.

If you are not at all musical, you can find your voice in many other activities; you can write poetry or prose, create works of art, design or invent something, join a political party or a campaigning group—there are many ways to express yourself. If you don't know where to start, take small steps and give yourself permission to make mistakes along the way. You may have heard this before, but Thomas Edison failed many, many times before he invented the light bulb. What an accomplishment it was and how fortunate for all of us that he did not give up!

So give yourself permission to speak out and find your niche in the world. Don't allow your Inner Critic to stand in your way. He will berate you and attack you with guilt for giving yourself the time and space to focus on your dreams. You may hear the same old script going round and round in your head once again, saying, "Don't draw attention to yourself. Who are you to make a statement? Don't give your opinions because no one is interested. Keep quiet and don't rock the boat."

Whenever you feel guilty for stepping out in a new direction, or feel inferior to the challenge ahead, you can be sure that the Inner Critic is whispering in your ear. Take authority over his lies and threats and reply to him firmly: "Nothing bad will happen if I express my true self. Good things are going to happen to me as I step out in faith and follow my passion."

If you don't know what your burning passion is, explore some possibilities. Make a date with yourself to try something different; sign up for a creative workshop or an evening class. Go to the theater, learn a new skill, join a reading group, or plan a trip – whatever excites you or intrigues you. Think about all the things you enjoyed as a child. What were your natural, innate gifts? Have you continued to develop these talents or have they been neglected over the years? Your unique gifting is still within you, waiting to be set free again.

Your journal will help you explore the possibilities and set goals. Make journaling a daily discipline and you will find your authentic voice.

## Journaling Power Prompts

Even if you aren't a musician and can't carry a tune, you probably find that music inspires you. Most of us have favorite artists, perhaps varying with our moods, and certain songs and albums transport us to particular moments in our lives. For example, if you hear a song that you associate with your senior prom, your first road trip, or your wedding day, you are immediately taken back there in your spirit.

Music can also inspire us, move us, or express feelings that we haven't yet put into words. Have you ever heard a song for the first time and thought: "I could have written those lyrics about my life right now?" Or perhaps you sometimes write down lines from songs that strike a chord with you (no pun intended)?

Music helps us connect more deeply with our emotions and opens us up to other forms of expression. You may find it helpful to select pieces of music and write in your journal while you are listening to them. You may wish to express yourself by writing lyrics and asking a friend to compose a melody, or perhaps you can write a song without any help at all.

## Journaling Exercise #1

Take the title of a song and use that as an opening for a journal entry. What represents how you feel at the moment? "Don't Worry, Be Happy," "Wild Thing," or "Un-Break My Heart"?

## Journaling Exercise #2

Find the lyrics of your favorite song and copy them into your journal. Write about the experience of reading or listening to these words. What emotions or memories do they bring to mind?

## Journaling Exercise #3

What song was playing on your cerebral iPod when you awoke this morning, or what song has been stuck in your head lately? Sing it out loud for your journal – and then free-write about it.

## Journaling Exercise #4

Write the following words down in your journal:

- Happy
- Romantic
- Angry
- Sad
- Lonely
- Excited
- Restless

Next to each adjective, write down the first song that comes to mind. Now, when you're feeling each emotion, you'll have a soundtrack to accompany your writing about it.

**#WriteON!**

# Create Write Now!

*I saw the angel in the marble and carved until I set him free.*

– Michelangelo

For twenty-seven years I've lived in my dream home, a beach house in Marshfield, Boston. My home is in a stunning location and has always meant a lot to me. I found it during Labor Day weekend, 1989. I was working in Duxbury, Massachusetts (after a series of posts in Washington, D.C., Pittsburgh, England, and Atlanta). I'd spent many weekends walking on the beach, searching for a home. I wanted a two-story house with a bedroom facing the Atlantic Ocean, and enough space to indulge my horticultural ambitions.

The first time I drove past my house I knew it matched exactly the home I had imagined and longed for all of my life. It had two floors and two bedrooms, and the master bedroom had two sets of sliding doors opening onto an east-facing deck. It was breathtaking! On the deck I could watch the sun rising over the Atlantic Ocean every morning. And there was a yard with enough space for the garden I'd always wanted. I was overjoyed to see that this ideal home was for sale! I wasted no time in acquiring it and moving in. In this beautiful location I could enjoy the best of both worlds; I would have a retreat from work and a home in a real community.

The reality of my dream home proved to be rather different from my intentions. In my consultancy years I was never able to relax and enjoy it—there just wasn't time. I never took a weekend off just for myself to enjoy the beach and the panoramic views. Deep down I knew I was missing out on having a well-rounded life, but I was so focused on my business that I ignored the cries from my heart.

I needed a diagnosis of MS to turn my life around. Once my body had made its feelings clear about my past career choices, my journal did the rest and pointed the way forward.

Through daily entries I explored alternative ways to make a living and connect with other people meaningfully. After a few years working in mutual funds, I decided I wanted to create a unique business that would mean something to me and to the world. So day by day, page by page in my journal, CreateWriteNow.com was born. It's an interactive journaling website with a community of followers and I run it from my beachfront home, providing a wealth of resources for fellow journalers. It enables me to have a balanced lifestyle and enjoy my superb beach location, while doing something I consider to be very worthwhile.

I write a blog (which I have opened up to guest bloggers) and provide lots of free information on many aspects of writing therapy. I have attracted thousands of followers and we have grown together into a fascinating community of like-minded people, all working hard to transform our lives through writing therapy. As well as the free resources I provide, I sell workbooks and courses that I've written myself – and I feel wonderfully, creatively fulfilled.

I invite my followers to take part in specific journaling challenges according to their needs on a regular basis, and these structured programs accelerate their growth in the areas that matter to them.

One example is the Weight Control Challenge. It is a twenty-eight-day program aimed at breaking negative thought patterns, improving food choices, and empowering weight loss. I devised this course and ran it quite recently with impressive results.

Part of the Challenge involved keeping a food journal. But it wasn't a typical calorie-counting roster; participants kept what I called a "holistic" food journal. Instead of just listing the foods they ate and working out calorific values, they wrote about how they were feeling in their whole bodies, as well as what was going on in their lives emotionally.

For instance, "I just ate 2.3 ounces of chocolate" would turn into "What's going on? Boy, I just noticed that every time it starts getting humid, it really affects my sinuses."

The important part of the Challenge was that people were sitting down and focusing on themselves. Even if it was just five minutes worth of "me" time, they would simply sit there and breathe and realize that they had an Inner Critic, or were listening to old, self-destructive tapes in their heads.

Many participants were new to the process and found it uncomfortable to begin with. It triggered bad memories or unpleasant feelings that they were accustomed to burying. But ultimately, the practice was fruitful, as they realized that they were "bigger" than the issues that were holding them back and causing them to reach for more and more chocolate. I was heartened when Challenge participants started flooding the Facebook group with positive, triumphant messages like, "I was going to have some potato chips to make myself feel better, but I took a minute to journal about it, and then decided I didn't really want them. As you can imagine, the weight has fallen off."

These positive comments give me great encouragement. With CreateWriteNow.com I am free to take risks as I develop my business, and at the end of the day, I am not stressed or exhausted, even though I work hard and make a profit. My creative enterprise is deeply rewarding.

Until I launched my website, I had no idea there was such an inspiring community of fellow travelers on the journey toward wholeness; getting to know them has enriched my life. I am meeting more people daily as I run my various courses.

When people sign up to a Challenge I set daily exercises in an eWorkbook format, and participants are encouraged to share their ideas and insights in an interactive Facebook workshop. Of course, not everyone wants to share their private thoughts, and it's entirely up to the individuals concerned to decide whether they want to do this.

I have produced courses and workbooks on many topics, including:

- *27 Days of Journaling to Health and Happiness*
- *21 Days Declutter Your Life Journaling Challenge*
- *24 Days Whole Health Journaling Challenge*
- *22 Days Life Transitions Journaling Challenge*

I'd like to introduce a few of my CreateWriteNow.com journalers now. Here are some snapshots from their journaling journeys that I have permission to share with you.

## Tara Pray's Journaling Journey

*My journals have always been the place where I could be the most free with my thoughts, feelings and ideas.*

*When I was an adult my journaling style changed significantly. Gone were my simple adolescent writings and instead what emerged were the struggles of a young woman trying to understand life, who she was and where she was going. My journals became the place where I started to process how I felt and why, the choices I was making and who I was becoming. My journaling became mature.*

*Journaling is my safe haven. It is the one thing that makes sense to me, when life leaves me feeling confused and lost. On the blank page I can write about things that reside in the deepest parts of me. When*

Mari L. McCarthy

*problems arise and I am not able to find answers just by thinking it through, I can go to my journal and write—and most times emerge with a solution.*

*My journals are not only for my struggles, but for my joys and triumphs, successes and dreams. I include prayers, great quotes I come across and titles of books I want to read. I write down things I heard that I want to remember, ideas for things to do or places to go, my poems and doodle drawings.*

*Today my journaling continues to be the one thing that helps sustain me. My passion for journaling inspires me to encourage others to write too. I have shared the love of journaling with my children and many others through teaching journaling writing in group settings. Journaling, I have come to believe, is the greatest gift a person can give to themselves.*

*Few things make my heart sing like a beautiful journal and a great writing pen. Wherever I go you are sure to find them in my bag.*

### Stephen Van Vugt's Journaling Journey

*I've been journaling since just after I left high school twenty-six years ago, largely to explore my own self-expression and find a voice. My journal is the best place I know of to go to and really discover what I'm thinking and feeling, and it helps me deal with anxiety attacks.*

*I can look at my feelings and thoughts, and evaluate them. I can analyze any incidents that have provoked anxiety and ask myself: is this event really so terrible?*

*I've also been using my journal to track my health and my progress as a runner. So I've been measuring my progress as I train every day for different races, and I also use my journal to celebrate when I've completed runs. I've completed a 5K, an 8K, and 11K run now. And my journal has really helped me make that transition.*

78

*I like to write my journal every night: I'm a Night Notes kind of guy, as Mari would say. And I find it's easier to wrap up that way. I have more to say when I come in at night and look back at the day. I review what happened, what I did, and what I felt, and I consider what I can do to make tomorrow even better.*

*I've had many "a-ha" moments with my journal. In 2010, I was searching for purpose in life. And after rereading my journals I was able to identify my priorities: focusing on and improving my marriage, being a better father, and looking for purpose at work as well.*

*In 2012 I suffered from a bout of depression, and writing in my journal was really helpful. I wrote down all my thoughts and fears, and it really helped me to get through those dark times. And I can look back on those entries now and know that although I had a bad time, I came through it.*

*I re-read my journals a lot. I like to go back every year and review what happened that year. I have a set of questions I ask myself at the end of every year: What did I learn? Who did I meet? How did I grow? And this process is really productive. It helps me to be stronger for the next year, just as writing Night Notes helps to make the next day better as I learn from yesterday's mistakes.*

## Nina Day Gerard's Journaling Journey

*Writing is in my blood. It's in my DNA. It's in my soul. I've been writing since I was a kid. That being the case, adding journaling to the mix just feels like working one of my many alternate writing muscles, along with poetry, fiction, short stories, novels, and scripts. (My first novel was called My Brother's Keeper).*

*I turn to journaling when I need to get quiet and reflective, when I need to go within, and most often when I'm working out a specific issue. This is how I first discovered Mari's workshops.*

*Journaling through specific issues and times of challenge opens thought and energizes our inner capability to find answers. We become open to possibilities that maybe we hadn't thought of before. Journaling can move us into a great place of listening.*

*I've done Mari's 27 Days to Health and Happiness Challenge on two occasions. The first time, I was feeling extremely out of balance in all areas, and needed to center myself. The second time, I felt completely trapped and creatively paralyzed by my living situation. It's critical for any artist to feel safe and inspired in the spaces in which they live and create, and they're often the same space.*

*I experienced significant insight both times, but the second time was especially powerful. It was as if I whispered my desire to the Universe and almost overnight, my desire had taken shape – my husband and I were moving out of the apartment we'd lived in for seven years.*

*Soon after that, we moved into the apartment we were ready for at that stage in our lives. It was only five miles from my husband's job (and equally close to the medical facilities we needed when my husband faced a health crisis the following year). Rather than being distracted by our surroundings, we were able to get settled in our new place and re-focus on our creative goals.*

*I believe that journaling is a powerful tool for everyone who is willing to invest the time in themselves. And journaling can be a beautiful addition to a writer's work in particular.*

## Jenny Beatrice's Journaling Journey

*I'm proud to say I am what Mari calls a journaling master since starting her journaling program in January 2014. When I started on the first course, entitled 27 Days to Health & Happiness, I had been thinking about journaling for some time, but I never had a structure. I wasn't able to get started, I was lost, and I wasn't sure what to write about. Mari's program really focused me on forming a journaling habit.*

*The topics had a progression to take you deeper and deeper into specific issues. Some of the topics were more relevant than others, but they were all important in learning about yourself.*

*Some people are afraid of the blank page and how to get started; I'm not. However, sometimes I'll only write three words, sometimes I'll write three sentences, or it might be three pages or more. And I think whatever needs to come out, in however many words, at whatever time, is really important to you, and it's all valuable in the same way.*

*I have numerous journals, and I write all over them. I don't have one that I keep. And I go by mood. Some of them black and very serious, and I seem to write my serious thoughts in those. Some are more colorful. Those seem to be my more positive thoughts. So I like to switch it up.*

*Every time Mari starts up her 27-day program, I raise my hand. I learn something new about myself every time, even though they're the same topics and I know they're coming. It's interesting to see the progression from where you started to where you're landing as the program goes along.*

*I really find Mari's Facebook group very valuable. The sharing is wonderful, and I enjoy seeing how people are progressing on their own journeys. Mari is very supportive. She always follows up with your comments, giving you suggestions, telling you to go right back to your journal and write to her, and look for the answers that you are seeking.*

*I really credit Mari's program in helping me recognize what my deep-seated issues were. And I was able to share them with important people who could help me, including my family, a counselor, and my friends, who were all very, very supportive.*

*Now I can't say that I always achieve the happiness I hope for every day, but the psychological benefits have been beyond my expectations. My number one personal challenge is to be more positive – I'm a glass-half-empty person. Sometimes I'm even a glass-totally-broken person.*

Mari L. McCarthy

*So I'm trying to write down positive things in my life. I feel that will help me manifest more positive things in my life by recognizing them. So in future I plan to focus more on gratitude, and thankfulness.*

<u>Joan Porte's Journaling Journey</u>

*I have been using journaling and some of Mari's techniques to work on issues where I feel stuck. One morning it occurred to me to write about my first memory (which most people have when they are about two or three years old) and I've found that not only can you gain valuable insights from this exercise, but it's not a one-shot deal: it can be repeated again and again.*

*I wrote about it once and then I returned to it and said: "Well, let me see if I can pull something else out of this." So I went back again, re-wrote the scenario as the heading, and then just started again with the new ideas that were coming to me.*

*And I wrote and wrote, and it was a completely different aspect to the experience. I was writing down the reasons why things were traumatic: this meant this with this person, and it meant that with that person. And I've done it three times now and I will probably do it again, because every time I look at this one event something new comes up about relationships and the past.*

These stories show how five different people use their journals to boost their creativity, actualize their potential, and meet life's challenges. There are many more testimonials at CreateWriteNow.com and I encourage you to check them out.

## Journaling Power Tips

Would you describe yourself as a creative individual?

When creativity is nurtured in a supportive environment, it is able to thrive and grow beyond your expectations. When it is blocked, on the other hand, it wilts and begins to fade with disuse. Your creativity can be stifled by a parent, spouse, or partner who is not supportive, or, worse, actively attacks your self-worth. Perhaps you were advised against taking a creative path and told to do something more sensible with your time or money. Even unintentionally, people can discourage us from being our true selves.

Sometimes we can be our own worst enemies too. We convince ourselves that we will never be an artist, writer, dancer (or whatever we would like to be in our heart of hearts) and we stay on the same old treadmill.

Perhaps in the past you started a creative project and then your Inner Critic showed up uninvited and shot you down in flames, leaving you demoralized and deflated. As we've discussed previously, the Inner Critic is the archenemy of creativity, because he is a perfectionist. In contrast, the creative process is messy and requires that you give yourself freedom to experiment and fail many times before you produce a spectacular, amazing result.

When you are obsessed with perfection, you are striving for an unobtainable goal. If you only want perfect, you won't be satisfied with good or great. This is paralyzing for your Inner Artist and will lead to creative blocking or abandoning your project altogether.

Julia Cameron wrote in *The Artist's Way*, "Perfectionism has nothing to do with getting it right. It has nothing to do with standards. Perfectionism is a refusal to let yourself move ahead. It is a loop – an obsessive, debilitating closed system that causes you to get stuck in the details of what you are writing or painting or making and to lose sight of the whole."

So be kind to yourself and develop a supportive environment for your creativity. This requires making space for some joy in your life.

Be prepared to nurture your Inner Child, the artist within you. Deliberately take yourself off on "play dates" such as visiting the cinema, theater, or an art gallery; photographing or sketching a landscape; walking in an area of natural beauty; or attending a creative workshop that interests you. If you like interior design, begin a storyboard; if you want to invent a product, brainstorm ideas. Allow at least one day every month for breaking free from your normal routine.

Everyone struggles with creative blocks from time to time, whether short-term or long-term, and it's important to develop your own strategies for unblocking. You will probably begin to spot the same blocks surfacing time and time again, and with practice you'll be able to overcome them and move past them. Think of it as clearing a pathway so that your ideas and talents can proceed freely.

## Journaling Power Prompts

Try these exercises to help you break free from perfectionism and unblock your creativity.

## Journaling Exercise #1

Think about something you've always wanted to try, but haven't because you're afraid of doing it badly or looking foolish. Imagine that you set aside those fears and gave it a try, not caring if you looked like a beginner and simply enjoyed the experience. Describe in detail what it would be like in your journal. Would it be fun, liberating, silly, humbling, nerve-wracking? What would you enjoy the most? For example:

*I've always wanted to take up swing dancing, but I am afraid I will look like an idiot and end up stepping on my partner's toes all the time. If I signed up for class today I would be nervous but excited. I love big-band music – it makes me want to dance. The teacher would teach us a few basic steps and break them down slowly so we could practice on*

*our own before partnering up. Other people around me would also look self-conscious, but someone would make a joke about having two left feet to lighten the mood. We would all make mistakes and laugh them off, and it wouldn't matter because we would be having a good time…*

How did it feel to be free to be a beginner? What else would you try if you allowed yourself to do it imperfectly?

## Journaling Exercise #2

Once you realize the power of your Inner Artist, the sky is the limit for what you can create. Novels, photography exhibitions, documentary films, original songs, designer clothes – just tap into your unique blend of talents.

The only drawback to being so creative is that it can all seem overwhelming when you try to decide how to get started.

If you want to record an album of folk songs, you may start worrying about recording equipment, record labels, performance venues, and marketing campaigns before you've even started to write your first song. Before you know it, you're so far ahead of yourself that even taking out your guitar or a piece of sheet music seems intimidating and you abandon the project before you've given it a chance.

So instead of always thinking of the big picture, take a different approach: start very, very small.

- Think of a project you are excited about starting. What does it involve? How does it challenge or inspire your inner artist? Write a short paragraph describing your overall vision. For example: "I want to start a line of handmade stationery. I have been experimenting with making cards and envelopes featuring my original designs, and I feel ready to start scaling up my efforts and making it into a side business."

- Review your summary of your new project and write down three small steps you can do immediately to move it forward. For example: "I will pick a name for my stationery line, start an online shop on Etsy, and sketch one new design for the first round of cards."

- Commit yourself to completing these steps in the next few days. Then repeat the process and complete three more steps, and so on.

## Journaling Exercise #3

Make a mental line-up of your creative blocks and how they affect your Inner Artist. For example, when you start working on a new painting, a little voice in your head gives you a running commentary on how well Tina from your master class is doing: "She just got her first solo show at a gallery downtown, you know. She got a rave review from that picky newspaper art critic, too. I bet she has buyers lined up for her work." And as you compare yourself to someone else, you feel swamped with feelings of inadequacy. Or as you write a poem, you tell yourself: "I'm crazy to think anyone will like my work. I don't have the right education to write poetry."

Now write a list of your creative blocks, or turn them into a page of caricatures. Name them, recognize them, call them out, and tell them they won't continue to have power over you.

Your list might look something like this:

- Jealousy – of others who are doing what I want to be doing

- Fear – of failure, judgment, or even success

- Guilt – I feel selfish and indulgent for spending time on creative pursuits

- Self-doubt – I don't know if my work is ever going to be any good

Keep doing your Morning Pages every day; this process makes you dig deep within yourself for the truth. Every morning, when you are pouring your thoughts out onto the page, you are gradually revealing your passion, pain, hope, and fear through your words. Keep going, and over a period of weeks and months you will begin to unearth your personal interior "map."

You will get to know yourself on a more profound level. The process will be disruptive at times, but it will show you where you are stuck and need to change. It will also be empowering and comforting, giving insight into your dreams and goals. And it's difficult to complain about a situation morning after morning, month after month, without taking constructive action – so you will move yourself forward.

I hope your journal has inspired you to do something creative – or at least to explore your possibilities. In the next chapter we'll approach the benefits of journaling from a scientific angle. Be prepared to be impressed!

#WriteON!

# The Proof Is In the Pudding

*To write about what is painful is to begin the work of healing.*
— Pat Schneider

So far in this book we've been looking at journaling in a very personal way, and seeing it very much as an individual journey towards health and wholeness. Our approach has been humanistic, but now we're going to change perspective and look at writing therapy more objectively.

My aim in this chapter is to highlight some of the influential studies carried out by research psychologists in clinical and laboratory settings, where the effect of therapeutic writing has been measured scientifically, recorded numerically, and analyzed statistically.

Scientists have asked the question "Does this really work?" and the answer is that it undoubtedly works for many people in more than three hundred studies. Writing can be a very effective therapy.

In this chapter I'll discuss some of the major findings in this area of work. I haven't tried to analyze all of the experiments carried out; such an undertaking is beyond the scope of this book. But I'll highlight a number of studies that have influenced current thinking within the scientific community. The pioneer in this field is James Pennebaker, whose work is mentioned frequently throughout this chapter.

As you read, remember that these experiments were carried out in laboratories or controlled settings. Usually when particular people are being studied, such as students with depression, or hospital patients with asthma, they are divided into groups. Some of the participants are placed into an experimental group and instructed to write about the traumatic events in their lives or about emotionally relevant topics. But another group of participants (a control group) are requested to write about non-emotional or trivial topics.

Because these controls are in place, researchers can identify whether expressive writing has had any impact. Without such controls it would be impossible to know if improvements in the experimental group were due to their writing, or down to random factors. So whenever I mention a study and allude to the experimental group or control group, you'll understand exactly what I mean (and if you've studied a scientific subject at an advanced level you will know all of this anyway. I apologize in advance if at certain points you think I'm stating the obvious).

This chapter is a little more academic than the rest of the book, but I want to give you lots of references so that you can look up the research if you wish. Alternatively, you can just skip over the studies quickly and get a broad picture of just how beneficial it is to write therapeutically.

## The Physical Benefits of Expressive Writing

Scientists have known for years that a trauma of any significance makes people vulnerable to sickness and depression – it can even precipitate death from cancer or heart disease. But almost thirty years ago, Pennebaker began his ground-breaking research into the area of healing from trauma.

Working with J.R. Susman, he found that people who talked about their ordeal, whether it was the death of a family member, a divorce, sexual trauma, or any another event that had significantly changed them, were better off than people who kept their experiences a secret.

Not talking about a trauma put people into a high-risk category for both major and minor illness, and they needed to see the doctor forty percent more often than those who openly discussed their feelings.

Further studies confirmed these results, as did the first-ever study about writing as a potential therapy. Pennebaker reasoned that if talking about traumatic events was helpful, then writing about them might also be effective.

Almost fifty students took part in the first writing experiment and agreed to write for fifteen minutes a day for four consecutive days (although they didn't know what they would be asked to write about). They were randomly assigned to two groups; one group wrote about "the most traumatic experience of my life" and the other group wrote about a non-emotional topic.

The students in the "traumatic experience" writing group wrote about all sorts of distressing experiences, and many were in tears. However, most of them continued to write for four days and reported that the experience of writing had been important to them on a profound level.

With the participants' permission, Pennebaker and his co-researcher S.K. Beall compared the number of visits made to doctors (due to illness, not routine check-ups) before and after the study. In the first four studies of this type, it was found that the students who had written about their traumas made forty-three percent fewer visits to doctors than those who had written about a non-emotional topic.

## Stress

Traumatic experiences cause stress, and there's no doubt that stress affects the immune system in humans and animals; it's a well-known biological fact. And it's something that's often observed in life. For example, it's common for people to become ill after they've suffered a bereavement.

The negative effects of stress are widely recognized, but most people don't realize that writing can help them to de-stress. Indeed, it's been reported that when people write or talk about traumatic events, they often show immediate signs of reduced stress. This can be measured by reduced tension in the facial muscles, lower blood pressure and reduced heart rate (Pennebaker, Hughes & O'Heeron 1987; Davidson et al, 2002).

This quick reduction in stress appears to benefit the immune system. Several studies have found that expressive writing enhances the performance of the immune system (Pennebaker, Kiecolt-Glasser & Glasser 1988; Lumley et al. 2011; Koschwanez et al. 2013) and some researchers have found that the benefits last for many months (McGuire, Greenberg & Gevirtz 2005).

Writing has been shown to help people suffering from many chronic illnesses, including asthma patients who showed improvements in lung function, and rheumatoid arthritis patients who had better joint mobility when tested (Smyth & Arigo 2009; Smyth et al.1999).

Writing has also been used as an intervention with cancer patients, and they reported feeling less pain, sleeping better, and functioning better during the day with fewer troublesome symptoms (Rosenberg et al.2002; De Moor et al. 2002; Henry et al. 2010; Low et al. 2010).

In another experiment, HIV positive patients who did some expressive writing had higher white-blood-cell counts than those who did not write. In this study, the experimental group showed an improved immune response similar to that seen in mono-therapy with anti-HIV drugs (Petrie et al, 2004).

Lupus patients have also been studied (lupus is a serious auto-immune disorder). Real gains have been documented for patients who were less fatigued in the three months following their writing therapy (Danoff-Burg et al. 2006). And patients with liver disease who used writing therapy were found to have healthier liver enzyme levels when tested in an experiment by Francis and Pennebaker in 1996.

The list of illnesses and complaints that are responsive to writing therapy as an intervention is a long one. In addition to all those I've already mentioned, patients with irritable bowel syndrome (IBS) have benefited, and so have women with chronic pelvic pain. The women reported reductions in pain intensity ratings after taking part in writing exercises.

But you don't have to have a chronic illness to benefit. Many studies have been carried out on healthy populations of young people, and after doing some expressive writing for a few days, they caught fewer colds.

## Psychological Benefits of Writing

We are holistic beings, so writing doesn't simply help our bodies – it helps us mentally too. Several studies have found that expressive writing facilitated better moods or fewer symptoms of depression (Spera et al, 1994; Pennebaker and Francis, 1996; Lepore, 1997). A further study found increased emotional wellbeing in those who wrote therapeutically (Park and Blumberg, 2002).

Sometimes people with anxiety and depression tend to ruminate (think repetitively about negative personal issues), and in 2006 an expressive writing study was carried out on college students known to be vulnerable to depression because of their medical histories. At the end of a six-month assessment period, their level of brooding and ruminating had fallen significantly.

Sometimes the gains from writing are intellectual, too. Quite a few studies have measured academic performance and found that students who did expressive writing performed better than control groups (Pennebaker, Colder, and Sharp, 1990; Cameron and Nicholls, 1998; Lumley and Provenzano 2003).

## Working Memory

Working memory is a technical term used to describe our ability to solve complex problems and attend to difficult tasks. If we are worried about lots of issues, including things that have happened to us in the past, it seems to affect working memory.

In one experiment, thirty-five freshmen were asked to write down their personal thoughts and feelings about coming to college, while at the same time another thirty-six students were given trivial topics to write about. There were significant improvements in the first group's working memory. In a follow-up experiment, researchers found that writing about a negative experience was more beneficial to working memory than writing about something positive (Klein and Boals, 2001).

In more recent studies (Dalton and Glenwick 2009; Frattaroli, Thomas, and Lyubomirsky 2011) students who did some expressive writing before their exams achieved better grades and reported better moods.

Psychologists carrying out research have several different theoretical perspectives on why writing helps with working memory. But it appears that writing about emotional stuff really does "clear the mind," whatever the mechanisms involved.

One theory is that memories of emotional or upsetting events tend to be fragmented and poorly organized. Such fragmented memories can rise to the surface very easily, appearing as unwanted and intrusive thoughts while we are trying to concentrate on other things. Because working memory is limited in its capacity, unwanted thoughts connected to unresolved emotional issues can be very distracting on a day-to-day basis.

In order to process these emotional memories, and "file them away" so that they are less intrusive, we need to explore how and why these stressful events happened to us. Expressive writing helps us to do this. As we gain insights into past traumatic events, we can transform fragmented memories into a story that makes sense to us. This helps us lay our most troubling memories to rest and move on. We are able to focus on the task at hand and live in the present.

## Sleep and Emotional Processing

Sleep is very important to physical and psychological health, and here too the benefits of writing have been revealed. Writing in the *Journal of Behavioral Sleep Medicine* in 2003, Harvey and Farrell reported on an experiment with poor sleepers, who had a tendency to lie awake worrying. The researchers tested the hypothesis that excessive thinking at bedtime was an attempt to process the emotions and hassles of the daytime. They hoped that writing would help the problem sleepers to carry out this emotional processing before they went to bed so that they could get off to sleep more quickly. This proved to be the case: Harvey & Farrell found that the participants who had been asked to do some Pennebaker-style journaling went off to sleep more quickly than those who did not write.

Many of the CreateWriteNow.com community find that writing at night helps them to sleep better, and I recommend Night Notes as an alternative or addition to Morning Pages. I will explain a bit more about Night Notes in the journaling tips section later in this chapter.

## Social Effects

Clinical and health psychologists have also found that expressive writing can help in social situations and help people to resolve conflict in their relationships. A study by Barclay and Skarlicki in 2009 required participants to write about injustices that they had experienced at work. The group that wrote freely about their thoughts and feelings reported higher psychological wellbeing and fewer intentions to retaliate after the writing exercise.

Writing may also improve people's confidence in social situations. In two studies (Pennebaker and Graybeal 2001; Baddeley and Pennebaker 2011) people were asked to write about traumatic experiences, and to wear a small tape recorder that recorded all their conversations on the days before and day after the writing exercise. It was discovered that after completing their writing, participants conversed more with others, used more positive language, and laughed more often and easily. It was as if writing made them feel socially comfortable.

People who journal regularly often say they feel they are handling their negative emotions more efficiently. In *Expressive Writing: Words That Heal*, James Pennebaker describes a group of middle-aged men who had unexpectedly lost their jobs in a high-tech industry. They were "the most angry, hostile, unpleasant bunch I've ever worked with," he said.

The men took part in an expressive writing study where one group was asked to write about their deepest thoughts and emotions about losing their jobs. The rest of the participants were asked to write about time-management strategies. Eight months after the study, fifty-two percent of the men who wrote about their emotions had new jobs, compared to only twenty percent of the group who wrote about time management (Spera, Buhrfeind, and Pennebaker 1994). Pennebaker concluded that the men who wrote about their deep feelings had benefited from the writing and that it had helped them to get past their experiences. They had not been compelled to tell their prospective employers how they felt abused by their last company and so had made a better impression at interviews.

"Writing helped transform these men from hostile ruminators into more open and accepting adults," said Pennebaker.

## Immediate and Longer-Term Effects of Writing

As we've discussed in earlier chapters, experimenters have discovered that writing about difficult and emotional experiences can sometimes cause distress or a negative mood while this writing is taking place. People may feel sad or angry, and shed a few tears. These effects usually wear off in a few minutes or hours. However, when the same people are followed up weeks and months later, there is evidence they have received long-lasting health benefits. These improvements can often be measured objectively by blood samples and other medical tests and are not simply based on the information given by patients, demonstrating that there is a material link between expressive writing and better health.

It's clear from the scientific work I've mentioned that writing is a powerful healing force in many people's lives. James Pennebaker himself has commented, "As the number of studies increased, it became clear that writing was far more powerful than anyone ever dreamed." That is not to say that every single person who tries journaling will be healed. There is no therapy around today that can claim a one hundred percent success rate, and writing is no exception.

In every study ever carried out, there are some people who benefit and others who do not, but the overall picture is encouraging and doctors in general practice are taking the results seriously.

In 2012 two general practitioners, Soul Mugerwa and John Holden, published a paper in the *British Journal of General Practice* entitled "Writing Therapy: A New Tool for General Practice?" While pointing out that it was unlikely to be a universal panacea, the authors said there was enough evidence to warrant full trials of writing therapy in primary care.

They concluded that expressive writing might help patients who did not want counseling or conventional psychotherapy.

"The next decade could see a useful new intervention for a variety of conditions that can be difficult to treat in general practice. Since writing therapy may help in a variety of problems, we may come to use it very widely indeed," the GPs concluded.

## Who Benefits Most From Expressive Writing?

Pennebaker says that all types of people benefit from writing; you do not need a particular personality or level of education to find healing. There is an indication that people who are out of touch with their own feelings may gain more from their writing than easygoing, self-reflective characters. Men often find it hard to express their feelings verbally, and there's a subtle gender difference showing that men may benefit from writing more than women, although the difference is a slight one. Studies have been carried out in many countries, and among different social classes, and it appears that nationality and social status are not very important: good results have been found for expressive writing all over the world and among individuals of the upper, middle, and lower classes.

## Theories About Expressive Writing

Psychologists have many different perspectives on human behavior and how the mind works, and it's not surprising that they don't all agree on exactly how expressive writing brings about healing. The theories are quite complicated and I'm going to attempt to summarize them in just a few sentences using everyday language. If you want a more precise and technical analysis I suggest you look up the primary sources, particularly if you are a mental health professional, doctor, or another professional with more than a passing interest in the subject.

First, I'd like to emphasize that the biological, psychological, and cognitive processes involved are complex, and the benefits of writing probably come from a combination of cognitive, emotional, and social processes, rather than from any one factor in isolation.

Here are some possible contributing factors:

## Emotional Catharsis

It may be that we get some relief from venting negative emotions when we write, a bit like opening a release valve and reducing the emotional pressure that's built up. This is an idea that Sigmund Freud proposed and he based his talking therapy, psychoanalysis, on it.

## Emotional Inhibition and Confrontation

Pennebaker has suggested that it takes a lot of effort to actively inhibit thoughts and feelings about traumatic events, and that this inhibition (in layman's terms, "keeping a lid on it") acts as a stressor on the body. Confronting the trauma by talking or writing about it is thought to reduce the physiological work of inhibition and reduce the stress on the body that might otherwise lead to physical or mental illness.

## Exposure

Sometimes the more we expose ourselves to traumatic memories (through talking or writing), the less they upset us, through a process called emotional habituation. It's a bit like getting used to handling a spider; after a while we get used to how it looks and feels and we don't react with fear or distress. This doesn't mean you have to write about the same event indefinitely, though. Write about it for a few days and then leave it for a while.

## Coherent Narrative Theory

As we write about our issues, we increasingly construct a coherent narrative, a story that makes sense to us. This is reflected in the use of "insight words" in our writing – for example, *I understand, I realize.* As we put a coherent narrative together we are processing our experiences, and this almost certainly helps us to heal.

## Cognitive Processing

As we have discussed before in relation to the Klein and Boals study, it may be that writing helps us organize and structure our fragmented emotional memories, improving working memory and helping us adapt to our past experiences. Organized memories appear to be less intrusive and less painful on a day-to-day basis.

## Conclusion

While it would be unrealistic to claim that writing therapy can help everyone, the data is impressive. Thousands of people have benefited from expressive writing in recent years, and that is only the tip of the iceberg. Most people are still unaware of the solid scientific evidence in favor of writing. Further publicity is needed so that the general population becomes more knowledgeable in this area.

Writing as a therapy has much to commend it. It is cheap, simple, and easily accessible to most people. The only "side effect" is its potential to change your life.

I firmly believe that journaling unlocks life-changing, trans-formative power. Pennebaker himself says, "Expressive writing is a self-reflective tool with tremendous power. By exploring emotional upheavals in our lives, we are forced to look inward and examine who we are."

I hope that this chapter has encouraged you to continue your writing practice, now that you know the evidence for journaling is scientifically validated and not just anecdotal and based on a few people's personal opinions.

Keep in mind that if journaling had been highly marketable, like a drug, millions of dollars would have been poured into researching it, and even more into marketing it. There would have been many more studies in existence than the three hundred we have to date. But journaling is a free tool, available to almost anyone, and there's no scope to patent it. That is why it is little publicized and many people are unaware of its transformative power. We need to spread the word far and wide about just how effective it is.

## Journaling Power Tips

Let's turn our attention now to the subject of Night Notes. They are a useful alternative or addition to Morning Pages. Night Notes are especially useful if you hate mornings or find it hard to get off to sleep at night.

Some people don't feel well first thing and it takes a long time for their brain to wake up properly. When they try to write Morning Pages they can't think of anything much to say. But the same people can rattle off three or four pages at night without any problem. So don't fight against your own body clock; try a different approach and do your reflective journaling in the evening. Use Night Notes as an opportunity to analyze what went right and what went wrong during the day and to re-group if necessary.

I mentioned earlier that in scientific studies, people who did some Pennebaker-style journaling went off to sleep more quickly than those who did not write. Harvey and Farrell suggested that insomniacs lie awake at night because they haven't finished processing the emotions and hassles of the daytime. They concluded that writing at night helped problem sleepers to carry out this emotional processing earlier in the evening so that they could get off to sleep more promptly. This is why Night Notes are perfect for certain people.

We may not always acknowledge it, but our brains are working flat out all day. At night they need time to decompress from all the thinking we make them do during waking hours. And this processing takes an hour or more. So have at least an hour of peace and quiet before you go to bed; play soothing music, have a relaxing bath – and write in your journal.

Therapeutic journaling at the end of the day is a way to clear the mind of thoughts and worries and to frame your day positively. Writing in your journal will help you process what happened during the day and let it go.

## Journaling Power Prompts

Use these prompts as a basis for writing Night Notes:

## Journaling Exercise #1 (to be completed in the evening)

What's on your mind? I'll bet that you can't do much about it now that it's bedtime, so write it down to get it out of your head and onto the page. Documenting any loose ends allows your brain to relax instead of having to remember it all night. Whatever it is, you can deal with it tomorrow.

## Journaling Exercise #2

What things did you accomplish today, big and small? What are you thankful for today? Write down as many things as you can. You might write, "Exercised for an hour," and "Weather was warm and sunny today." Reflecting on what you did accomplish today (rather than what you didn't), and what blessings you have (rather than those you don't), will help you contentedly drift off to sleep. Over time, this gratitude practice will get you in the habit of framing the events of your day in a positive manner, no matter what happens.

## Journaling Exercise #3

Close your entry with a brief reflection or prayer that expresses any blessings or wishes you have on your mind. Writing a quick reflection or prayer is a powerful ritual for closing out the day intentionally and letting it go. As you shut your journal, let a sense of closure and peace come over you. As you close your eyes, let your mind go quiet, and let your muscles relax. Know that your day is complete.

**#WriteON!**

# Having It All

*You don't get harmony when everybody sings the same note.*
— Doug Floyd

Journaling has brought harmony into my life – literally and figuratively. Let me unpack this statement.

In a very literal sense, therapeutic writing helped me re-discover my long-lost ambition to sing; I followed my dream and became a recording artist. But journaling has also brought harmony to my life in a figurative way, helping me to achieve equilibrium.

I've learned to balance responsibility with fun, my need for solitude with my hunger to connect, and so much more. As I've progressed on my journaling journey, I've seen my life come into harmonious balance.

And among my most important journeys has been the transition from "or" to "and." Let me explain this vital concept.

## From "Or" to "And"

Before journaling, I used to think in terms of Or. I thought I had to choose between two favorable options because I believed they were in conflict. I did not believe I could have them both, or "have it all." For example, I assumed it was impossible to have time as well as money.

Through journaling, I've been learning to think, feel, and live in terms of And—being able to have two things that I thought were mutually exclusive. For example, it's possible to care for your body while also being mentally productive, and it's possible to meet your own needs while also earning a good living.

I've learned that I can move through morning, noon, and night, all week long, feeling balanced and satisfied in all the right ways, without a nagging sense of deprivation.

Understandably, most of us believe we must make big sacrifices to achieve satisfaction in our lives. And we accept as a normal casualty of life the painful sense that a lot is being given up in order to attain the things we want.

Journaling has taught me to tune into my health, live with compassion for myself, and move through life with a sense of balanced harmony – in very measurable ways.

## The Idea of "Or"

Before I set off on my journaling journey, I held certain beliefs that felt indelible and intractable. It wasn't that I could not let go of these beliefs: I just didn't really think about them. They were part of life's received wisdom, which I assimilated blindly. I thought I had to make the following choices:

## Body "Or" Mind

I was neglecting the link between my body and my mind. I took it for granted that if I was thinking hard but physically uncomfortable, that was acceptable. On the other end of the spectrum, if I was lying on the beach or getting a massage – treating my body well – I felt guilty because I wasn't "getting things done." And if my body got so relaxed that my mind seemed to go blank, guilt washed overhead and slammed into me like a giant wave.

I'd sit in front of my computer after work, hunched over, my fingers cramping up and a sliver of a headache forming at both temples. I wanted a glass of water but did not feel like I could stand up and fetch one from the kitchen: the time did not feel right. I told myself I would do it in a minute or five, once I'd finished planning the next morning's meeting. So many people are like that when working, and I'm sure that you've experienced it yourself. We tend to ignore our bodily discomfort or take a pill instead of getting to the root of the problem. For instance, if you're getting headaches often, perhaps you need to consider whether stress or a lack of sleep could be playing a role, instead of popping Advil and hoping that the headache doesn't persist or come back later.

Now, I'm not saying we should spend all day always and only in touch with our bodily functions and feelings. That would be ridiculous; we would have to have no engagement with the outside world, where responsibilities are imposed on us every single day. It's not a sin to pop painkillers when your quadriceps hurt after an unusually strenuous weight-lifting class.

But the problem of Or arises when we feel that being physically uncomfortable while mentally productive, or taking care of the body while giving the mind a break, are alternatives from which we're forced to choose.

My journal has taught me that it is possible to achieve balance between my mind and body. In fact, it's not only possible, but very, very important. If I am not feeling a sense of harmony in my mind **and** in my body, I write about it in the pages of my journal. And most of the time, after a few pages, the solution reveals itself somewhere between my brain and my heart, the pen and the paper. And boy, does it ever feel good to sit down and write the next morning, after I've resolved the issues affecting my body **and** mind. Through journaling, I've learned never to sacrifice one for the other.

105

## Time "Or" Money

Before my journaling journey took off, I believed that in order to make a living I was happy with, I would have to sacrifice "me time." In the company I'd built, I felt I was running on a tightrope (in a power suit), tensing myself in order to maintain that precarious position. I felt vulnerable to falling far, far downward at any moment.

Constantly, I told myself: "Push through, go-go-go, take setbacks in stride, just keep moving."

I was always "on," in work mode and wearing the proverbial "thinking cap." Even when moving forward felt like walking on that tightrope (with no safety net in sight), I silently sang this "go-go-go" refrain to myself. I sang it so often, with the notes reverberating through my tired body, that it became a habit and then a lifestyle.

As I became more and more successful, and more and more was expected of me, I gave myself less and less permission to take time out. I had no down time, so there was never an opportunity to tune into my thoughts and feelings, or pay attention to my body and how it might be reacting.

The rat race traps many people like this. They believe they must consecrate nearly all of their time to earn the kind of money they want or need. Of course, this isn't just an illusion in their heads: jobs demand seemingly endless hours sometimes. It may seem counterintuitive, but the antidote to this pressure is found in journaling.

## Freedom "Or" Productivity

Before I discovered journaling, while I was still running my business, I thought that "productivity" meant being overscheduled. I was so busy that each day was regimented down to the very last minute. I felt emotionally and creatively trapped.

My daily writing therapy revealed just how trapped I felt; the pressure was taking its toll. I did not feel free, deep inside my heart – and there were physical ramifications, too. I felt tightly bound to my daily schedule: "Must down food within five minutes, must spend just ten minutes getting ready and then speed down the highway, no breaks during the day to stretch my legs allowed." This tightness manifested itself throughout my body. My back was always sore, my neck in knots, my stomach tossing and turning.

Each day when I sat down to journal, I would discover how constricted I had been feeling, and I would get in touch with my desire to feel looser and freer.

As I've described in Chapter 6, journaling literally brought me a way to make a living and connect with others in a meaningful way. Through writing about my options in depth I came to a place where I could take a chance on something that felt right: CreateWriteNow.com.

And now, through this creative enterprise, I can fulfill myself expressively, intellectually, and with every part of my being, right down to my little toe. I am free to take risks, free to reap the rewards of connecting with other people, and at the end of the day, it doesn't feel like work – even when others would call me "productive."

The fact that my business, with its workbooks and courses for sale, produces items and turns a profit is icing on the cake, and reaffirms the power of staying true to your heart. It's a far cry from those days when I was crashing into walls of my home, click-click-clicking on my desktop computer while I slumped over it – hungry for healthy food, thirsty for a big glass of water, and craving sleep or time to watch the waves on my beach.

Mari L. McCarthy

## Creative Expression "Or" Facing Reality

Before I began journaling, I thought that in order to be successful and in touch with reality, I couldn't feel creatively curious or fulfilled. I pushed away any inklings of wanting to express myself creatively, so that nagging inclinations (what if I wrote an essay or belted out a song?) wouldn't interrupt my day-to-day functioning as a business-woman. I was convinced I could not have creative expression as part of my life in the real world.

Journaling showed me the opposite was true. My journal affirmed that I was a whole being, and my desire for creativity was important. Because of my insights gleaned through journaling, I explored my creative inclinations instead of ignoring them. And very shortly afterwards, I was able to throw myself into my new singing career.

## Journaling Power Tips

I hope these examples have helped you understand what I'm getting at here: the whole Or thing is just plain wrong. Instead, it's all about And. Journaling taught me I could have all of these supposedly contradictory things, and I could have them all at once.

Sometimes it has felt like life was magically transforming for the better all on its own, as I diligently turned up every day to journal by hand. What was happening, in fact, was that the journaling was a journey of discovery, and my practice was showing me that how I felt mattered. I realized I deserved to have a full and balanced life, and my journal not only showed me that it was possible to get what I needed to live harmoniously, but also showed me how.

Sometimes I didn't even know I was feeling out of balance in certain respects, but by the time I'd finished a mere three pages of writing, the lack in my life would reveal itself clearly. And my journaling practice told me it was worthwhile getting what I needed, even if this was just an incredibly restful night's sleep.

Journaling brought about a sense of balance in my life. Once I understood this, reveled in it, and developed it more and more strongly through my daily practice of writing, pretty much every minute of my life started feeling like a joyful song.

So let me encourage you to use your journal to explore the critical issue of lifestyle. Look closely at the balance between mind and body, time and money, freedom and productivity, creativity and facing reality. Consider how to change Or to And.

Look at the tension between time and money in your life. Write about how you have no time to write or be creative. Your journal, I have no doubt, will help you to find ways to open up your day. That might mean thinking about your time at work differently, so that your actions feel more your own and in line with what you feel in your heart, or finding ways to streamline processes to get what you really need: precious minutes, seconds, and hours.

Journaling may show you how to scale back hours while still making big money. Or it may reveal how the hours of work needn't be so painful, so you can make even more. When consulting your journal, it's important to acknowledge that while money is vital, your time is also very, very important. A balanced relationship between time and money is possible to achieve.

I understand it is not always possible to make your source of productivity into something so freeing. If the practice of productivity in your life is making you feel trapped, and it doesn't seem obvious how to break free, try to insert some freedom into your productivity in creative ways.

For some people, taking figurative ownership of their work helps. So when a task is assigned to them at work, they think: This project is mine, and it's up to me to actualize its potential. This shift in thinking alone can effect a powerful and transformative feeling of freedom.

On the other hand, maybe you can fit an activity you love into the middle of your productivity. For instance, if you really hate cleaning out your closet and have been dreading doing it for months, tell yourself the task is on your terms: you can take a break and go for a run or eat a slice of chocolate cake whenever you feel like it.

Get to know the real, authentic you and create the healthy, balanced lifestyle you need. The answers will not appear overnight; it is a lifelong journey to get to know your true self, to realize who you are at your core and what drives and inspires you in life. It takes a great deal of courage to embark on this path of self-discovery and remain open to what you find – your fears and insecurities, dreams and talents, quirks and struggles – but it also provides great rewards. When you embrace your strengths and face your challenges, you create a strong foundation for a happy and fulfilling life. You unlock your potential to be your true, authentic self.

## Journaling Power Prompts

Your self is your gift to the world, and it evolves through experience. For example, at the age of twenty-two you may describe yourself as a student, a friend, an artist, and a traveler. At forty-five, you may think of yourself as an entrepreneur, a parent, a musician and a member of a community. Your identity will grow and change throughout every phase of your life, and this is something to be appreciated and embraced, rather than resisted. With your journal, explore the question "Who am I right now?"

## Journaling Exercise #1

Think of who you are in terms of different areas in life that are important to you. There will probably be some overlap in these different categories, but try to come up with five to ten areas in which you may exercise different facets of who you are. For example, these might be: work, family, social life, art, hobbies, travel, and spirituality.

- Open your journal and write down each category, leaving about a half page of space in between each. Answer the question, "Who am I right now?" for each important area of your life. This can simply be a list of words that come to mind or a few detailed paragraphs. Be honest and describe how you really see yourself – without shaming or blaming. Maybe you think you are good at your job, but it doesn't relate to what you are truly passionate about. Maybe you are proud of being a parent who gives both unconditional love and necessary limits to your children. Perhaps you are such a loyal and supportive friend that you sometimes have trouble saying "no" and disappointing the people you care about.

- Read what you've written in each section, and reflect on the significance of each area of your life. Write a brief statement – no more than two sentences – that sums up who you are right now. Think about where you seem to be thriving, and where you seem to be struggling.

## Journaling Exercise #2

How you see yourself is often influenced by how others see you. For example, if you are perceived as funny and charming in a social situation, you may find yourself chatting and joking easily with a group of total strangers. But if you are perceived as boring or tedious in that same situation, you might become self-conscious and nervous, clamming up or talking too much to try to impress others.

In a classic social psychology study from Dr. Mark Snyder and colleagues, the researchers found that people can sense how others view them and then start exhibiting those expected behaviors. This self-fulfilling prophecy is something we have all experienced. Other people's expectations have a powerful effect, and it's easy to let them influence – consciously or unconsciously – how you feel and how you act. Other people sometimes view us negatively, and put labels on us that are not helpful. Your journal helps you challenge both your self-perceptions and the messages you have received from others.

So now revisit the areas of your life that you wrote about in Journaling Exercise #1:

- Do the same exercise, but this time describe how key people see you in each area. What are their perceptions and expectations of you? How do these views influence your self-image and behavior?

- Free-write about your thoughts on your responses from yesterday and today. Was anything surprising to you? How do you think who you are differs from how others see you? Is there anything you want to change about these expectations?

## Journaling Exercise #3

Do you ever daydream about the places you want to go to, the activities you want to try, or the goals you want to achieve? When was the last time you let your imagination run wild with lofty plans? In this exercise, you'll explore the ideas that give you butterflies in your stomach or make you smile from ear to ear.

- Set a timer for thirty minutes. Think about everything you want to do over the next five or ten years (or even over your lifetime). Make a list of everything that comes to mind that you get excited about. What would you be glad you tried, no matter what the outcome?

• When the timer goes off, keep writing if you're still on a roll!

## Journaling Exercise #4

Now explore the idea of living honestly and authentically.

• Write about what it means for you to live an authentic life. When do you feel you are being most true to yourself? Which people or circumstances most encourage you to embrace who you are?

• Write about the biggest challenges to being true to yourself. What part of your identity makes you feel vulnerable? What are you afraid to reveal to others for fear of being judged, ridiculed, or misunderstood? How does hiding this part of your identity keep you from living a full and authentic life? How can you make small steps to let this part of yourself be seen?

We've covered a lot of ground in this book, and I've passed on tools and techniques for journaling as a holistic healing therapy. Now it's time for action!

Setting goals and reaching them is the key to success in any area of life, and your journal can help you do that. So get ready for the final chapter! I am going to give you a simple blueprint for setting specific, measurable, and realistic goals. Get focused, think BIG, and believe for the best!

#WriteON!

# Higher and Higher, Baby

*You are never too old to set another goal or to dream a new dream.*

– C.S. Lewis

I hope by now you've decided to create the happy, healthy life you want to live, through the power of journaling.

In this final chapter I'd like to encourage you to plan the next five or ten years of your life, using your journal to write a vision and an action plan for success. When I refer to future success, I mean your definition of success and not anyone else's. Journaling will help you define your own core values and what matters most to you in life; writing everything down will help you achieve your goals in bite-sized steps.

I believe everyone has a purpose and a destiny. You may have discovered yours already, and if so, journaling will help you move forward in your own field of endeavor. If you are a little confused about your direction in life, however, there are exercises in this chapter to help you find clarity.

First let me share my own experiences of using my journal to set goals (a goal is a dream with a deadline to make it happen).

As I said in Chapter 5, I am a recording artist, and my journal was important on my vocal journey. I always wanted to be a singer, but singing in public was a big challenge for me. I analyzed my fears by writing them down. My journal was a safe place to reveal these fearful emotions, and as I wrote it all down in black and white, I was able to identify my negative-self-talk and challenge it with positive affirmations.

With each CD I have recorded, I have written in my journal at length using the free-writing (stream-of-consciousness) technique, and during the act of writing I've noticed sometimes that phrases just "drop into" my mind. I write them down, and ask myself questions, such as "I wonder what this is all about, and how is it connected to my music?"

I have received many ideas like this and have a special name for them – universal messages. For example, my latest CD is called *Lady With a Song*, and one day this title just showed up in my Morning Pages.

I feel that the consistency of writing every morning (without fail) unleashes the Muse within me. If you have any difficulty with this concept and find it esoteric, you may prefer to think in terms of releasing creative ideas from your unconscious mind and making them conscious. The more you write, the deeper you dig, until you find a hidden treasure.

My journal plays a big role in all of my decision-making. I use it for every aspect of goal setting and action planning, and I ask myself a series of pertinent questions and then free-write the answers. For example:

What is a realistic date or deadline for this action?

Does this course of action make sense? Does it feel right?

Who do I want to help me with this task?

I break the whole process down into steps. I have a productive working relationship with my journal; it's like a friend or counselor and it doesn't pressure me.

As I explained earlier in this book, I have worked with my journal on health-related goals too.

When I decided to come off all my prescription drugs, it was a big decision. I wrote about the issues in my journal, particularly the fact that the drugs were making me sick for two days each week and were not a cure (but were merely settling some of my symptoms). I decided that, for me (I am not advocating this course of action for everyone), it was the right decision to stop my drugs; they were not worth the financial and emotional cost.

## Planning the next step

I chose to become my own health advocate, and so in my journal I am always asking myself: "What's the next step toward my goal of whole health?" The answer doesn't always appear overnight, but over a period of time, a resource will show up. For example, I discovered a scientific article that said that certain foods containing gluten might exacerbate MS, so I began to eat gluten-free alternatives and have noticed an improvement in symptoms. It's helped my stomach and digestive system and has had a positive impact on my auto-immune functioning. Similarly, going dairy-free has improved a long-standing problem with sinus congestion.

Another goal I set was to sleep for seven or eight hours every night. I came up with an action plan in my journal to help me wind down in the evening. I analyzed my evening activities and discovered I was stimulating my brain too much. I wrote a list of alternative activities to help my brain wind down every night, including writing Night Notes as a "dumping" exercise to clear my mind of anxious thoughts before bedtime. I suffer with much less fatigue in my nerves these days because my diet, sleeping pattern, and exercise routine have been improved through the process of goal-setting and action-planning with my journal.

However, where I really notice the difference is in the big picture of my life. Thanks to my daily pen-to-paper Journaling Power practice, I am the happiest, healthiest, and most authentic version of myself that I could possibly be, and this shows up in many areas. There has been a huge amount of positive change.

For example, I strive to use all of my talents and be my best, rather than suffering, struggling, and sabotaging myself at every turn. I have fun living in the present, setting and getting to my goals. I work with non-traditional healthcare resources and I eat mindfully, choosing the foods that nourish and satisfy my body; I think positive thoughts like "Yes, I can" and "It will all work out."

## Journaling Power Tips

You can see big changes in your thought and behavior patterns too. Journaling is a brilliant way to get focused and create a vision for your life. You can build a picture in your journal until you can clearly envision what you want to happen, as if it had already taken place. A vision is central to your success.

If we look at many of the most influential people in the world, we can see that they were driven by a vision for how things could be – and then they worked tirelessly to make that dream a reality. They didn't necessarily do it all alone, but they focused on the big picture and inspired others to take hold of it too. Here are some famous examples from history:

- In 1961 John F. Kennedy spelled out his dream that the U.S. could land a man on the moon within a decade. Some scientists thought it was impossible, but the president inspired people to try to meet the deadline, and in 1969 Neil Armstrong became the first human to walk on the moon.

- In the 1970s Steve Jobs had a vision of putting computers into the hands of ordinary people. As the CEO of Apple, he was staggeringly successful at doing just that.

- The prominent Catholic nun and Nobel Peace Prize recipient Mother Teresa was driven by her calling to feed the hungry and clothe the naked in obedience to Christ's teaching. She gave physical and emotional support to hundreds of homeless and sick individuals living in the slums of Calcutta from 1948 until the 1990s.

- Civil-rights activist Martin Luther King Jr. made a famous speech in 1963 outlining his vision for racial equality in the U.S. and mobilizing non-violent protesters to see huge progress in this area.

We can't all be as influential as these famous figures, but these examples illustrate a general principle – the vision comes first, and it inspires action. If you think about it, everything that has ever been created began as an idea in someone's imagination, whether it was an Apple computer, a mission to the moon, a social movement, a number-one hit record, or a best-selling novel. The same principle applies in every person's life: to make something concrete happen, we have to begin in the invisible realm of the mind and spirit.

"Without a vision, the people perish" is a Biblical proverb that is often quoted in many spheres of life because of its profound truth. Many people will admit that living without clear goals is de-motivating, while having a strong vision is empowering. When goals are written down and made measurable, and when we believe we can achieve those dreams, things happen.

So how can journaling help with this?

Journaling takes us to the sacred space where we can connect with something bigger than ourselves – the place where dreams are made. Depending on your spiritual or philosophical beliefs, you may interpret this space as somewhere you can meet with God, encounter your Higher Self, or access your own subconscious desires, to gain a clear picture of your direction and ultimate destiny in life.

You may experience this as a coherent vision, or just a general sense of where you want to make some changes and see some improvements, perhaps in areas like health, finances, career, or creative and artistic development.

Wherever you are in your journey, you will find that writing down a vision and some specific goals and action steps speeds up your progress and makes success much more attainable. In one study at Dominican University, participants who wrote down goals and action steps and shared them with a friend (and sent weekly updates) were on average thirty-three percent more successful in accomplishing their goals than people who just kept their plans in their head.

The problem is that we can get so caught up in our hectic, day-to-day existence that we lose sight of the bigger picture. We don't leave ourselves enough time to pause, reflect, and refocus, or to ask ourselves: "Is this what I really want? Am I heading in the right direction? What do I really want to do?"

And even if you have formulated a long list of goals you would like to achieve someday – running a marathon, starting a photography blog, or hiking Machu Picchu for example – you may not have taken concrete steps to reach them.

So in the final section of this book, you'll find a series of exercises aimed at helping you clarify your vision, goals, and action plan for the future. You can break down your goals into bite-sized chunks and take decisive, courageous action to reach them. You may feel a little fear as you leave behind the familiar landscape of your past life and head for new vistas, but I want you to know that you deserve success and that it is achievable, one step at a time.

## Journaling Power Prompts

These prompts are designed to take you through the whole process of discovering your vision, setting goals, and producing an action plan. This is the most extensive section of journaling prompts in the book and it will take a week or two to work through all of the steps, but it's a worthwhile investment in your future happiness.

## Journaling Exercise #1

Before you do this exercise, center yourself by listening to some classical music, meditating, or saying a prayer.

Turn to a blank page in your journal, and write a date that is exactly five years ahead. Think about how you'd like your life to be five years from now. What are you doing? Who are you with? What is going on in your life? Where do you want to be?

Don't be afraid to think ambitious thoughts; just go with the flow.

Write a page or two about your life five years from now, and – here's the crucial part – write it in the present tense, as if it's already happened.

For example, if you want to become a teacher, you would picture yourself in the classroom and imagine what's happening around you. You might write:

*I'm teaching history, and the children are working really well. They are so engaged in the lesson and they look happy and focused on the task. The head teacher has been watching and has just handed me a feedback form that says she's very impressed with my teaching skills.*

Try to cover the major areas of your life, work, relationships, health, and so on.

When you've written down your vision, review it.

Was there anything in it that surprised you? Do you feel a little clearer now on where you want to be in five years' time?

When you're completely happy with your vision, read it out loud to yourself. Speaking out loud releases creative power and helps your subconscious mind to act on the information you have given it.

## Journaling Exercise #2

Now take the vision you wrote for Exercise #1 and brainstorm in your journal:

How might I get from where I am now to the place I see myself five years from now?

Make a list of possible ideas. For the example we've already discussed (becoming a teacher) you might write:

- *I'll research the universities that provide teaching courses and check out the entry requirements.*

- *I'll speak to some of the teachers I know and see if they have any advice for me.*

- *I'll read some books and watch some videos about teaching.*

- *I'll volunteer to help out in my local school to get some practical experience with children.*

Write a short list for every major area of your life; then ask yourself:

- Which ideas are you most excited about? Which do you think will be the most challenging? Which do you think will be the most rewarding? Explore these questions in your journal, then circle the goals you would most like to see realized.

## Journaling Exercise #3

Write your top goals (identified in Exercise #2) at the top of a fresh page in your journal.

Are these goals related? Do they have any common themes, values or background?

Now spend some time thinking about each goal individually. Get to know each goal better by using these questions as a starting point in your journal:

- Why did you select this goal? What about it do you find most appealing?
- What interests does it engage? What other experiences does it draw from?
- What values does it support? How do these values fit into your overall approach to life?
- How do you envision the process of working toward your goal? What do you want to learn, and how do you want to grow?
- How do you think others might be affected or influenced by you working toward and achieving your goal? Who do you think will be the most supportive?

Close each of your goal entries with one or two sentences summarizing the main ideas you want to keep in mind as you go forward. You can refer back to this if you need support or motivation in the future. If for example, one of your main goals in the next five years is financial security, you might write: *Building a strong financial foundation is the best way I can safeguard my family's future and ease my current tension and worry.*

## Journaling Exercise #4

Now have a think about your environment and whether it is friendly toward your goals. To be successful and handle challenges, you must create an environment where you can thrive. Think about your work situation, mental and physical health, your personal support system, and your attitude toward change. If you were a plant, you'd need nourishing soil, sunlight, and water to become healthy and strong. As a human, you need certain resources too; support from other people, money, education, and so on. So take a close look at your surroundings and work out what is needed to improve this environment.

Are you heading in the right direction to reach your goals, or have you been focusing on another path? What kind of support and resources do you need?

Here's a drawing exercise to do in your journal:

Take out a pen or some colored pencils, and draw a picture of yourself surrounded by the most important elements that shape your life (don't worry about your art skills). You may love drawing, and want to make detailed depictions, or you may want to use simple symbols (such as several hearts to represent people in your family). Do whatever makes sense to you, and try to represent all aspects of your life.

For example: • *Demanding but satisfying job* • *Supportive family* • *Struggles with anxiety* • *Love of trying new things but fear and insecurity about taking big risks* • *Limited finances*

When you have finished your drawing, try to view it objectively. What would you say, as an outsider, about this person's environment? What factors seem healthy and conducive to setting goals? Which seem unhealthy or detrimental? Why? Write your observations in your journal.

## Journaling Exercise #5

Think about some of the fears, obstacles, and challenges that may have held you back in the past and answer these questions in your journal:

- How long have you been thinking about this goal? Does it come to mind often? When it does, how does it affect your emotions?

- What do you think is the biggest reason you haven't yet accomplished it? What are some of the smaller reasons?

- Have you tried to work toward this goal in the past? If so, what happened? What made you stop?

- Do you feel that fear has hindered your progress? What is your biggest fear? In your mind, what is the worst-case scenario if your fears are realized?

For example: *It's been twenty-five years now since I set my sights on completing the Appalachian Trail hike, and I've toyed with the idea of doing it a few times in the past, but I've never gotten past the initial brainstorming phase. Time has always been a challenge; either I was in school or working, or it was tough to take time off. I'm also intimidated by the physical fitness and endurance the hike requires. I wonder if I've waited too long and I'm getting too old to do it.*

## Journaling Exercise #6

Taking the first step toward an important goal can feel intimidating. Take a deep breath and relax: it's normal to feel a little overwhelmed at the beginning of a new journey. Remember that you have the power to dictate your own pace, make your own rules, and set your own milestones. Pursuing what is important to you is empowering and exciting, and it all begins with one small first step.

For this exercise, put the big picture aside and focus only on the immediate future. This will help you make progress without being paralyzed by your long-term to-do list. Write your goals at the top of a blank page of your journal. Now brainstorm five to ten simple actions you can start and complete in the next few days. For example, if one of your main goals is to go to graduate school, you might write:

*First steps:*

- *Do initial online research on academic programs that fit my interests (time: an afternoon).*

- *Go to the library and check out books on the fields I'm interested in and grad school admissions. Start reading these books (time: two hours).*

- *Call or send emails to friends, acquaintances, and family members who have experience in my field of study or know people who do. Ask if they would have time to chat with me (time: two hours).*

- *Print or bookmark academic calendars and admissions guidelines for the programs that interest me. Mark dates on my calendar (time: one hour).*

Underneath your list, write down your thoughts on how you feel planning these first steps. Are you relieved, nervous, stressed, or ecstatic? Do you feel as if these steps are reasonable and achievable? If yes, write down a date by which you would like to finish them. If no, go back to your list and tweak it so that it sets realistic expectations.

## Journaling Exercise #7

In this exercise, you'll make a plan for managing fear and frustration. These are powerful emotions; they can hold you hostage, cripple your decision-making skills, and prevent you from moving forward with your goals. When you are challenging yourself to venture outside your comfort zone and try something new, you will inevitably have moments where you feel scared or discouraged and ready to quit, but it is important to know how to cope with those feelings and keep going.

- Write about a time when you were faced with an obstacle that derailed your progress toward a goal. What were you trying to achieve? What happened to throw you off course? How did you react? Why? For example: *A few years ago I was trying to get myself back to healthy habits: eating better, exercising more, and, most importantly, quitting smoking. I wanted to quit and was determined to do it without the aid of patches or gum or anything, but I kept slipping up. I'd have a stressful day at work and sneak out for "just one" cigarette or go to a party where everyone else was smoking and fall into old habits. Every time I slipped, I would beat myself up over it and feel really guilty, and it got to the point where I figured, "What's the point?"*

- What did you learn about yourself and your needs from this experience? How do you think you could have reacted differently for a better outcome? Did you eventually reach this goal? What were the secrets to your success? For example: *I did end up quitting smoking, but it took a lot of false starts for me to realize what I was doing wasn't working. For a long time, I thought if I had enough willpower and discipline, I could kick the habit on my own. I eventually realized that I needed more outside support and accountability to stick with my plan. I talked to my doctor for advice, started weaning myself off nicotine with the patch, and rallied a group of friends to quit along with me. It was still hard and took a long time (and some more slip-ups), but it was much more realistic once I had set up a safety net to help me when I struggled.*

- Now think of another situation when you faced fear or frustration while working toward a goal, but you were able to stay on track and overcome the challenges. How did you react differently than in the first story? What actions were key to your success? For example: *At the beginning of my career, I was offered a great job in my field. The only problem was that the job was three thousand miles away from my family and anyone I knew. I had never moved far from home before, and I was nervous, but the job was a wonderful opportunity and I felt I had to take it. The first few months in my new city were up and down – exciting but also very lonely – but I made myself promise that I would stick it out for at least a year. I ended up staying for five years and growing a lot professionally and personally.*

• What did you learn about yourself and your needs from this experience? How can you use these lessons when faced with future challenges? For example: *I learned that sometimes you have to make yourself uncomfortable or even unhappy for a period of time to be able to have some of the most rewarding and life-changing experiences. In this case, I had to make a leap of faith and do something that scared me, forcing myself to give it a fair shot for a set period of time. It would have been much easier to give up after a month and head back to what was safe and comfortable, but because I had set a timeline for myself, I had to stick it out, and it was worth it in the end.*

• What are the main takeaways from what you have just written? What factors help you reach your goals more easily? What tricks, tips or pieces of advice can you give yourself for when the going gets tough? Write yourself a cheat sheet or pep talk to read when you need extra encouragement and support.

## Journaling Exercise 8

Setting and accomplishing major goals is not an overnight process. It takes hard work and perseverance, as well as passion and enthusiasm, to figure out what is important to you and to create a plan of action to pursue it. So now, make notes on the following:

• Do you have a current time-management strategy? If so, what works well? What do you find most challenging? What time of day is best for you to work on personal projects?

Brainstorm some strategies that will allow you to make the most of your precious spare time. For example: *If I go with the flow and don't plan anything, I end up never making time for projects. I do better when I look at a monthly calendar as well as my daily schedule and block off small periods of time each day. I also work full time, so I'm pretty exhausted when I get home in the evening. Saturdays or early mornings on weekdays are my most productive times.*

- Since your time is so valuable, it is important to be able to rank which tasks deserve your attention first and which can be placed on the back burner for the moment. Do you feel comfortable with prioritizing what to work on and when? Do you often struggle with balancing the different demands in your life? What helps, and what doesn't? Record your observations in your journal. For example: *I often want to do everything all at once, and it's hard for me to accept that I have to do a little bit gradually over time. I think it would help to make a big chart, list, or timeline of what needs to happen to reach each of my goals. That way I'd have a visual record of everything and can put the pieces of the puzzle together more easily.*

- It's helpful to establish habits that encourage your responsibility and commitment to your goals, and an outside perspective can often be just the push you need. What would be the most useful accountability strategy for you – enlisting a friend to help you with the planning process, sending a weekly email update to a family member, or having a casual check-in with your spouse over Sunday morning coffee? What will motivate you to stay on track and not be an unnecessary burden? Create a customized plan that works for you. For example: *I need someone who is fair but tough to ask me for regular updates on my goals. One of my best friends is an event planner and very organized. If I ask her to check in with me every time I see her, I'll be more likely to stay focused.*

• It's easy to fall into a classic trap when you set a new goal: early excitement and a flurry of activity… then a long lull and a slower pace, eventually leading to a loss of motivation and the abandonment of the project. So now consider: How can you keep moving forward? What can you do to stay motivated and enthusiastic about your objectives? Write a list of tips for yourself. For example:
  • *Take at least one small step toward my goal every day, even if it takes just five minutes*
  • *Daydream about the day when I finally reach my goal (and throw a huge celebratory party)*
  • *Skip one TV show if I think I don't have enough time*
  • *Remember that an occasional misstep does not equal failure*
  • *Be kind to myself – growth is hard*

• Now personalize your goal toolbox. Add anything else that will help you as you work toward your goals.

That's it! You've done all the preparatory work, like a gardener removing all of the stones and weeds from a flowerbed that is ready to be planted. It's time to transform your vision into a reality. Good luck – and remember, no one else can do what you do in quite the same way. You deserve success and it's within your reach.

Stay committed to a daily pen-to-paper journaling practice and positive action, one day at a time. You can create the happy, healthy life you want to live!

#WriteON!

Mari L. McCarthy

# References

Almond, S. (2012) Why Talk Therapy is on the Wane and Writing Workshops Are on the Rise *New York Times Magazine* March 23

Baikie, K.A. & Wilhelm, K. (2005) Emotional and Physical Health Benefits of Expressive Writing *Advances in Psychiatric Treatment* 11, 338-346

Baddeley, J.L. & Pennebaker, J.W. (2011) The Expressive Writing Method in Research on *Writing Approaches in Mental Health*, eds L.L'Abate & L. Sweeny, 23-35 UK Emerald

Barclay, L.J. & Starlicki, D.P. (2009) Healing the Wounds of Organizational Injustice: Examining the Benefits of Expressive Writing *Journal of Applied Psychology* 94(2) 511

Cameron, J. (1995) The Artist's Way: A Course in Discovering and Recovering Your Creative Self *Pan Books*

Cameron, L.D. & Nicholls, G. (1998) Expression of Stressful Experiences Through Writing: Effects of a Self-Regulation Manipulation for Pessimists and Optimists *Health Psychology* 17 84-92

Dalton, J.J. & Glenwick, D.S. (2009) Effects of Expressive Writing on Standardized Graduate Entrance Exam Performance and Physical Health Functioning *Journal of Psychology* 143(3) 279-292

Davidson, K., Schwartz, A.R., Sheffield, D. et al (2002) Expressive Writing and Blood Pressure in The Writing Cure: How Expressive Writing Promotes Health and Emotional Wellbeing eds. Lepore, S.J, & Smyth, J.M) 17-30. Washington, D.C., *American Psychological Association*

Frattaroli, J., Thomas, M. & Lyubomirsky, S. (2011) Opening Up in the Classroom: Effects of Expressive Writing on Graduate School Entrance Exam Performance *Emotion* 11(3) 691-696

Gortner, E., Rude,S. & Pennebaker, J.W. (2006) Benefits of Expressive Writing in Lowering Rumination and Depressive Symptoms *Association for Behavioural and Cognitive Therapies* (Elsevier Ltd)

Hanlon, E. (2011) The Art of Fiction Writing: Or How to Fall Down the Rabbit Hole Without Even Knowing *Smashwords ed.*

Harvey, A.G. & Farrell, C. (2003) The Efficacy of a Pennebaker-Like Writing Intervention for Poor Sleepers *Behavioral Sleep Medicine* 1, 115-124

Henry, E.A., Schlegel, R.J., Talley, A.E., Molix, L.A. & Bettencourt, B.A. (2010) The Feasibility and Effectiveness of Expressive Writing for Rural and Urban Breast Cancer Survivors. *Oncology Nursing Forum* 37(6) 749-757

Jackson Nakazawa, D. (2015) Childhood Disrupted: How Your Biography Becomes Your Biology, and How You Can Heal *Atria Books*

Klein, K. & Boals, A. (2001) Expressive Writing Can Increase Working Memory Capacity *Journal of Experimental Psychology* 130, 520-33

Koschwanez, H.E., Kerse, N., Darragh, M., Jarrett, P., Booth, R.J. & Broadbent, E. (2013) Expressive Writing and Wound Healing in Older Adults: A Randomized Controlled Trial *Psychosomatic Medicine* 75 (6) 581-590

Lepore, S.J., (1997) Expressive Writing Moderates the Relation Between Intrusive Thoughts and Depressive Symptoms *Journal of Personality and Social Psychology* 73, 1030-1037

Lumley, M.A., Leisen, J.C., Partridge, R.T., Meyer, T.M., Radcliffe, A.M., Macklem, D.J. & Granda, J.L. (2011) Does Emotional Disclosure About Stress Improve Health in Rheumatoid Arthritis? Randomized, Controlled Trials of Written and Spoken Disclosure *Pain* 152 (4) 866-877

Lumley, M.A. & Provenzano, K.M. (2003) Stress Management Through Emotional Disclosure Improves Academic Performance Among College Students with Physical Symptoms *Journal of Educational Psychology* 95 641-649

Mugerwa, S. & Holden, J.D. (2012) Writing Therapy: A New Tool for General Practice? *British Journal of General Practice* 62: 661-663

Palumbo, D. (2012) Dealing with Your Inner Critic *Psychology Today* May 19

Park, C.L. & Blumberg, C.J. (2002) Disclosing Trauma Through Writing: Testing the Meaning-making Hypothesis. *Cognitive Therapy and Research* 26 597-616

Pennebaker, J.W., Colder, M. & Sharp, L.K. (1990) Accelerating the Coping Process *Journal of Personality and Social Psychology* 58 528-537

Pennebaker, J.W. & Evans, J.F. (2014) Expressive Writing: Words That Heal *Idyll Arbor*

Pennebaker, J.W. & Susman, J.R. (1988) Disclosure of Traumas and Psychosomatic Processes *Social Science and Medicine* 26, 327-332

Pennebaker, J.W. & Beall, S.K. (1986) Confronting a Traumatic Event; Toward an Understanding of Inhibition and Disease *Journal of Abnormal Psychology* 95 274-281

Pennebaker, J.W. & Francis, M.E. (1996) Cognitive, Emotional and Language Processes in Disclosure *Cognition and Emotion* 10, 601-626

Pennebaker, J.W. & Graybeal, A. (2001) Patterns of Natural Language Use: Disclosure, Personality and Social Integration *Current Directions in Psychological Science* 10 90-93

Pennebaker, J.W., Hughes, C.F. & O'Heeran, R.C. (1987) The Psychophysiology of Confession: Linking Inhibitory and Psychosomatic Processes *Journal of Personality and Social Psychology* 52, 781-793

Pennebaker, J.W., Kiecolt-Glaser, J.K & Glaser, R (1988) Disclosure of Traumas and Immune Function: Health Implications for Psychotherapy *Journal of Consulting and Clinical Psychology* 56 239-245

Petrie, K.J, Fontanilla, L., Thomas, M.G., Booth, R.J. & Pennebaker, J.W. (2004) Effect of Written Emotional Expression on Immune Function in Patients with HIV Infection: A Randomized Trial *Psychosomatic Medicine* 66, 272-275

Rosenberg, H.J., Rosenberg D.S.D., Ernstoff, M.S. Wolford, G.I., Amdur, R.J, Elshamy, M.R, & Pennebaker, J.W. (2002) Expressive Disclosure and Health Outcomes in a Prostate Cancer Population. *International Journal of Psychiatry in Medicine* 32(1) 37-53

Smyth, J.M., & Arigo, D. (2009) Recent Evidence Supports Emotion-regulation Interventions for Improving Health in At-risk and Clinical Populations *Current Opinion in Psychology* 22(2) 205-210

Smyth, J.M., Stone, A.A., Hurewitz, A. & Kaell, A (1999) Effects of Writing About Stressful Experiences on Symptom Reduction in Patients with Asthma or Rheumatoid Arthritis: A Randomized Trial *Journal of American Medical Association* 281, 1304-1309

Spera, S.P., Buhrfeind, E.D. & Pennebaker, J.W. (1994) Expressive Writing and Coping with Job Loss *Academy of Management Journal* 37 722-733